ADDRESSING RACISM AND ABLEISM IN THE CLASSROOM AND TEACHER EDUCATION

Addressing Racism and Ableism in the Classroom and Teacher Education centers and elevates narratives of special education teachers of color, an overlooked and underserved population in public education, as a vehicle for analyzing the tensions of race and disability. Special education teachers of color, who work and may themselves live at the intersections of these complex identity constructs, are uniquely positioned to develop effective approaches to countering racism and ableism. This book offers five critical case studies of special education teachers of color, whose replicable practices span preschool through high school classrooms while also holding urgent implications for teacher education programs. Building toward an original framework that synthesizes DisCrit and Culturally Sustaining Pedagogies, these narratives refuse deficit readings of disability among students of color and instead prepare teachers to model collective joy and pride in their identities.

Saili S. Kulkarni is Associate Professor of Special Education at San José State University, USA.

Theory to Practice in Critical and Social Justice Education
Paul C. Gorski, Series Editor

Addressing Racism and Ableism in the Classroom and Teacher Education
Case Studies of Special Education Teachers of Color
Saili S. Kulkarni

ADDRESSING RACISM AND ABLEISM IN THE CLASSROOM AND TEACHER EDUCATION

Case Studies of Special Education Teachers of Color

Saili S. Kulkarni

NEW YORK AND LONDON

Designed cover image: cover art by Dr. David Connor

First published 2026
by Routledge
605 Third Avenue, New York, NY 10158

and by Routledge
4 Park Square, Milton Park, Abingdon, Oxon, OX14 4RN

Routledge is an imprint of the Taylor & Francis Group, an informa business

© 2026 Saili S. Kulkarni

The right of Saili S. Kulkarni to be identified as author of this work
has been asserted in accordance with sections 77 and 78 of the
Copyright, Designs and Patents Act 1988.

All rights reserved. No part of this book may be reprinted or
reproduced or utilised in any form or by any electronic, mechanical,
or other means, now known or hereafter invented, including
photocopying and recording, or in any information storage or
retrieval system, without permission in writing from the publishers.

Trademark notice: Product or corporate names may be trademarks
or registered trademarks, and are used only for identification and
explanation without intent to infringe.

ISBN: 978-1-041-10189-5 (hbk)
ISBN: 978-1-041-10190-1 (pbk)
ISBN: 978-1-003-65378-3 (ebk)

DOI: 10.4324/9781003653783

Typeset in Sabon
by Apex CoVantage, LLC

This book is dedicated to my beautiful son, Adhyaan. Adhyaan, you are everything I never thought possible. Your name, "to rise up," embodies everything we hope for in a more just, anti-ableist, and anti-racist world.

CONTENTS

Foreword   *xi*
Leigh Patel

Acknowledgments   *xiii*

Introduction   1

Background 2
Exploring the Tensions of Disability and Race 3
Importance of Special Education Teachers
   of Color 5
Book Overview 6
References 9

1 Understanding Racism and Ableism in Teacher
   Education Through Special Education Teachers of Color   12

Teachers of Color 13
   Recruitment and Education of Teachers of
      Color 14
Special Education Teachers of Color 15
   Early Research on a Diverse Special Education
      Workforce 16
   Recent Research on Culturally Sustaining Special
      Education Teacher Education 18

viii Contents

Recent Research and the Experiences of Special
  Education Teachers of Color 18
Teacher Education and Special Education in the
  California Context 20
  Special Education Credentialing Process 21
  Data on Special Education Teachers of Color From
    California 22
DisCrit Framework 23
  Narratives of Special Education Teachers
    of Color 25
  Organization of the Book 26
References 28

2   LaVeda: A Black, Female Preschool Special
    Education Teacher Building Classroom Community   32
    With Contributions by LaVeda Harris

    *Background and History: Teaching Where You
      Live 34*
    Integrating Connection and Representation 36
    *Supporting Behavior and Communication
      Universally 39*
    *Cultivating Joy in the Early Childhood Special
      Education Classroom 42*
    Concluding Thoughts 44
    References 46

3   Loriann: Integrating Disability and Race via a
    Restorative Lens in Elementary School   48
    With Contributions by Loriann Casillas

    How I Became a Special Education Teacher 49
    Challenges of Special Education Teaching 49
      Responding to Challenges 50
    Meeting Loriann (Saili's Perspective) 51
    *Restorative Justice Practices for Students of Color
      With Disabilities 52*
      Honoring Student Voice 55
      Restorative Justice Lens 57
      Resistance to Ableism and Racism 58
      The Need for Community Efforts 59

Contents **ix**

Conclusion 60
References 60

4 Samuel: Navigating Identity Alongside Disabled
Students of Color in Middle School   62
With Contributions by Samuel Bland

Background and History 63
  Challenges of Special Education 65
Imposter Syndrome 66
Navigating Identity 68
Sample Lesson Plan 70
Conclusion 76
References 78

5 Joanna: Multiply Marginalized Disabled Students'
Discipline Disparities in Middle School   80
With Contributions by Joanna De Leon Gaeta

Background 81
Challenges With Special Education 83
Behavioral Observations and Challenges 84
Discipline Disparities Among Male Minority
  Students 86
Humanizing Practices for Male Minority
  Students 86
Conclusion 88
References 92

6 Ashley: Unlearning Racism and Ableism Alongside
Disabled Students of Color in High School   93
With Contributions by Ashley Highsmith-Johnson

Background and History 94
  Challenges With Special Education 95
  Representation 96
Unlearning Internalized Racism and
  Ableism 97
Unlearning Racism and Ableism With High School
  Students 97
Conclusion 100
References 102

x Contents

7 Grappling With Racism and Ableism in Special
Education: Special Education Teachers of Color and
Resistance   103

*Tensions With Special Education and Teacher
    Education Curriculum 104*
*The Case for Disability-Centered Culturally
    Sustaining Pedagogies (DCCSPs) 104*
*Actively Building Resistance and Cultivating Joy
    With Multiply Marginalized Disabled Students of
    Color 105*
Moving Forward: Resistance Not Resilience 108
    Deinstitutionalize Special Education 109
    Focus on Resistance Not Resilience 110
References 111

Appendix A   *114*
Appendix B   *119*
About the Authors   *121*
Index   *123*

FOREWORD

DisCrit—the purposeful division of racism from ableism, when, in fact, racism cannot function, literally cannot exist, without ableism. This is the starting point, the grounding, and the heart of this book.

And if that weren't enough, this book exemplified the oft-repeated phrase that nothing any individual does is simply that person's singular achievement. We understand, learn, and unlearn with company. The chapters in this book feature many partnerships in a time when the term itself is used in neoliberal ways, acting what Sara Ahmed might describe as a nonperformative: claiming a partnership without actually being in an ongoing, consensual relation paradoxically prevents partnerships from fulminating organically. Not here, not in this book. Instead, Kulkarni's long-term and ongoing relationship with teachers of color who work with students in special education reaches beyond both two-dimensional ideas of partnership and provides a deeply needed and fresh take on "representation."

In this book, you will meet both Kulkarni's obvious commitment to interrogating oppression-laden narratives in favor of narratives that create possible futurities. You will also meet special education teachers of color. Because Kulkarni's approach is deeply steeped in ongoing "right" relation. This means that she shares stories of complexity that she has been given permission to share from the basis of working, learning, and unlearning alongside the teachers profiled and speaking in this book. So, this book takes us well beyond the importance of representation of, especially, Black teachers in the field of special education. Kulkarni weaves narratives from her co-researchers, the teachers she's often connected to through university-based coursework, to beautifully complicate what

xii Foreword

representation can mean. It can be, as Kulkarni illuminates throughout the book, that "I am not the only one," and it can also be made to shoulder an inappropriate amount of incremental change as sufficient.

The stories in this book invite readers to consider, reconsider, learn, and unlearn that a simplistic formula of representation is both necessary and insufficient. I can easily imagine this book being a school-wide read in any teacher education program. People will be uncomfortable as they learn, from the stories and societal analysis that Kulkarni provides, that dismantling the inseparable conjoining of racism and ableism is no small feat because of how pervasive it is. Everything from school-based ways of organizing who is deemed to have a disability is turned, necessarily, on its head to understand dis/ability in constant dynamic with the context of other people, place/space, objects, and the histories we all bring with us when entering a classroom. I can imagine scores of white upper-middle-class female teachers, still the overwhelming majority of teachers, wondering what their role should be and productively listening and reading this book harder. It is meant to unsettle a great deal and does so beautifully through story. Kulkarni manages a deft feat in this book: she both underscores the importance of teachers of color being mirrors, windows, and sliding doors, as Rudine Sims Bishop taught so beautifully, and makes us deeply contemplate just how far representation can take us. She also is one of the brightest lights to highlight the individualism in focusing on singular identities. Befitting this book, based so strongly on intersectional analyses, Kulkarni masterfully agitates just how far we can pursue intersectional resistance and intersectional futures if we confine understanding racism and ableism as things that happen to individuals at the expense of the population-level pattern.

I hope you read this book and share with me a deep appreciation for Kulkarni and her interlocutors' use of story to invite us into some obvious failures of schooling as well as the complexity of potentially being the "solution" as teachers of color. There are clear implications and ways to move differently in this book, but we only get there by the nuance that guides us throughout the book.

Leigh Patel

ACKNOWLEDGMENTS

The making of this book would not have been possible without the village of support that I received from colleagues, friends, and family. The first thank you needs to go to my husband, Tushar, for his enduring support during the writing of this book. He has been my constant source of support and care and has been the rock that holds our family together. Next, I would like to thank my parents, Sunil and Suneeta Kulkarni, and my sister, Shefali Kulkarni, for their support and encouragement as I worked to get this book out into the world. While they don't always understand what it is I do, they are constantly positive and eagerly celebrate my work.

Along the writing path, which was often circuitous, I was fortunate enough to have several colleagues support me as chapter editors. In order of chapter, this includes Dr. Marcos Pizarro, Dr. Luis Poza, Dr. Amanda L. Miller, Dr. Jason Laker, Dr. María Ledesma, Dr. Peg Hughes, and Enimai Villavan-Kothai for her style edits. Also, thank you to Dr. David Connor for the beautiful cover art and Dr. Leigh Patel for the kind foreword to the book. Special thanks to Dr. Phillip Boda, Paul Gorski, and the team at Routledge, who helped me turn around a difficult situation.

The authors of these chapters and I worked collectively and sought to reimagine education for multiply marginalized disabled students of color. Their experiences and dedication to our youth are unparalleled. Their stories highlight the complexities of a system of special education teacher education and schools that continue to perpetuate racism and ableism, and yet each of them continues to offer us with beautiful voices of resistance and activism both inside and outside of the classroom. I am forever indebted to them for collaborating on this project. Thank you, LaVeda, Loriann, Samuel, Joanna, and Ashley.

INTRODUCTION

Narratives facilitate structures. The stories that individuals tell about themselves, their people, their nation, other people, and success or failure all have material force in the shape and functions that institutions perform in society.

(Patel, 2019)

In her book *Disability Visibility*, Alice Wong shares that she didn't grow up seeing the stories of disabled people, especially those who were not white and male, ever being highlighted. Wong (2020) shared that she wanted to (1) see the stories of disabled people highlighted with respect to the present and past, (2) hear from the stories of everyday people rather than the exemplar, and (3) increase the diversity of disabled people and their stories represented in the mainstream. Stories have the power to bring in people who share and simultaneously those who don't share particular experiences.

Over the past six years, I have had the privilege of listening to the stories of a number of special education teachers of color. We conversed about their work in classrooms, preparation to become teachers and earn credentials, and early experiences as students of color and, sometimes, disabled students of color in US public schools. In addition to what they shared as a deep appreciation for being able to tell their stories, each teacher noted that they didn't see a lot of people like themselves: teachers of color working to support students with a broad range of students with identified disabilities in a variety of classroom contexts from racially, culturally, and linguistically nondominant backgrounds. In fact, most didn't see teachers of color

DOI: 10.4324/9781003653783-1

2 Racism and Ableism in the Classroom and Teacher Education

and/or with disabilities in any context: growing up, in their teacher preparation programs, or at their school sites.

I resonated deeply with what these teachers shared. As a former special education teacher of color, I also had very few teachers of color *at all* growing up, and there were only a few special education teachers of color in my credential program. Additionally, I was sometimes one of just a few teachers of color working at my school sites, despite working in a district with a large number of students of color. Navigating special education teacher education, I remember feeling isolated, alone, and frustrated at having to be one of the few individuals pushing for an intersectional framing of disability. Even without the deep understanding of theories that informed racialized experiences of education (e.g., critical race theory and later DisCrit; Annamma et al., 2013) until graduate school, my lived experiences and work in classrooms pushed me to conceptualize disability and race as interdependent.

My aim is that this book brings hope, connection, and validation to special education teachers of color who have experienced some of the same feelings that I and other special education teachers of color face(d) navigating spaces that weren't designed for us. I start this chapter by sharing a little bit about my own journey in the field of special education, then describing some of the tensions of bringing together race and disability in authentic and intersectional ways, and conclude with a brief summary of the book and include narratives of special education teachers of color.

Background

For the past six years, I have worked as a special education teacher educator at two public, four-year institutions designated as Minority-Serving Institutions (MSIs). My current institution, San José State University, was the flagship institution for the California State University system, the largest state university system in the United States. Prior to the Civil War, San José State University was called the State Normal School and served as an institution to train and educate teachers in California (SJSU History, n.d.). It is perhaps fortuitous, then, that I am a teacher educator and research teacher in California, at the institution that first began educating teachers in the state, and that my work across special education and disability studies seeks to challenge conceptions of the normative center of schooling.

Working as a special education teacher in Oakland public schools, I became starkly aware of the challenges of racism and ableism faced by disabled students of color. During my first years in the classroom, I was surprised by how segregated students of color with disabilities[1] were from general education settings and the deficit language and approaches by which students were being educated. Teachers, staff, and administrators were quick to label my multiply marginalized disabled students as deficient or impose labels of disability upon students of color who presented minor behavioral challenges in general education. Conceptually, I now know these to be unfortunate yet common practices in public schools across the United States (Farley & Taeuber, 1974). These observations of practice motivated me to pursue graduate studies and begin thinking more deeply about how teachers develop and sustain beliefs about race and disability and how these beliefs translate into their practices in schools.

When I started my doctoral work at the University of Wisconsin–Madison in the field of special education, I began to feel a tension in the descriptions of multiply marginalized disabled youth through a special education lens. These descriptions were often infantilizing or erased students' individual voices and experiences. It was through interdisciplinary work that married teacher education and disability studies and later DisCrit (DisCrit) that I started to find the integration of more critical perspectives on race and disability.

It was through these perspectives that I was able to explore teachers' beliefs about race and disability. I first explored these beliefs through the context of an international fieldwork opportunity that allowed pre-service teachers to complete a portion of their fieldwork in East Africa (Kulkarni & Hanley-Maxwell, 2015). I shared caution for such experiences, which, in some cases, reinforced white savior mentalities among teachers and some deficit perspectives on disability as a lack of capacity. To delve deeper, my dissertation explored how beliefs about race and disability were informed and enacted by California special education teachers and how these contributed to retention or attrition decisions (Kulkarni, 2015). This early work on teacher beliefs and practices grounded my interests to help prepare teachers to critically examine race and disability intersections through praxis. My work with teacher candidates and future teachers has always been to undo racism and ableism and support teachers, especially teachers of color, in navigating how whiteness and ability operate interdependently in P-12 schools. These aims of my work draw directly from my teaching experiences in Oakland, coursework and opportunities in graduate school, and my own identity as a woman of color, first-generation South Asian American, and person with invisible disabilities (Kulkarni, 2022a).

Exploring the Tensions of Disability and Race

Horace Tate reminds us to be watchful of what is happening to what has been built and be willing to destroy it if it no longer serves a purpose (Walker, 2018). We must think, then, about what we would be willing to destroy in the name of reimagining or recreating special education and teacher education to *completely* address the intersections of disability and race. Annamma and Morrison (2018) explain that we need to dismantle dysfunctional classroom ecologies. As a way to begin this, my colleagues and I write that we need a DisCrit-informed curriculum of teacher education, one that recenters disabled people of color as knowledgeable, upends harmful practices, and recognizes historical and current contexts in the lives of multiply marginalized disabled people of color (Kulkarni et al., 2021).

Indeed, much has been written about the intersections of disability and race (Annamma et al., 2013; Erevelles, 2014; Harry & Klingner, 2014), the ways in which it translates into P-12 classrooms (Migliarini & Annamma, 2020; Love & Beneke, 2021), and the challenges of adequately integrating both of these identities (Artiles, 2011, 2013), yet a true reconciliation of both identities intersecting and overlapping and the authentic representations of disability and race continue to elude teacher education (Kulkarni et al., 2021). Additionally, some disability categories, especially those that include significant or complex support needs, have been ontologically erased (Nusbaum & Steinborn, 2019).

Colleagues who challenge deficit-based narratives of race in the research and practices of teacher education often miss or superficially mention disability as an identity marker without a deep understanding of the ways in which race and disability interact and intersect (Boda et al., 2022). And, unfortunately, researchers who have produced progressive work on the education of students with significant and/or complex support needs (and their teachers) have not meaningfully addressed race and the racial tensions of this work (Miller, 2020).

Scholars such as Bettina Love (2019), for example, include brief discussions of disability and the school-to-prison nexus, school violence, mental health, and disabled girls of color (Annamma, 2017) but need to also address how abolitionist teaching addresses the everyday ableism endured by multiply marginalized disabled children and youth. Furthermore, how are "those who are dark" with complex support needs envisioned in freedom dreaming and abolition? How does disability status coupled with race impact school perceptions of multiply marginalized disabled youth via an abolitionist teaching framework? Grappling with these complexities requires additional attention to the identity of disability as it intersects with race.

Conversely, the field of special education has often relied on definitions of diversity that highlight disability as a marker of difference, and in some cases deficit, without an intersectional analysis (Pugach et al., 2021). One of the greatest challenges of scholarship on disability is that it often does

Introduction **5**

not include a racial analysis, and therefore disability is defaulted to represent *white* and disabled unless otherwise stated (#DisabilityTooWhite; Bell, 2010). This also erases the important perspectives that communities of color hold with respect to disability. For example, within special education, there is a push to uphold the "ableist myth of independence" (Chatterjee, 2018), where many communities value interdependence and connectedness. Additionally, without a focus on intersectional disability justice, scholars are likely to miss the critical contributions to special education, disability studies, and critical race studies that stem from the disability activist community (Sins Invalid, 2017).

Across these tensions is an additional need to center narratives as a way of providing first-person accounts of critical experiences. Annamma's (2017) work on disabled girls of color in the school-to-prison nexus, David Connor's (2008) narratives of disabled high school students of color, Cioè-Peña's (2021) narratives of mothers of emergent bilingual students labeled with disabilities, Miller's (2020) paper on disabled girls of color with complex support needs, and narratives that center families (Sauer & Rossetti, 2019) and multiply marginalized students with disabilities (Waitoller & King-Thorius, 2022) are all essential to decentering whiteness and re-centering race and disability.

Without more critical conversations about the intersections and tensions of bringing together race and disability, each of these constructions becomes a casual nod to the other. In critical general education scholarship, there is an erasure of the ways in which ability and disability are used as a tool of distinction and division. Furthermore, there is an ontological erasure of the identity of disability (Nusbaum & Steinborn, 2019) from spaces that purport critical and racial justice scholarship. Conversely, in disability studies and special education, race is either tokenized through language (i.e., using terms like culturally sustaining pedagogies or culturally responsive pedagogy interchangeably while not drawing either term into direct practice) or rendered invisible through scholarship (Kulkarni & Parmar, 2017) and practices (Klingner & Edwards, 2006). A deep understanding of how disability and race work interdependently is essential for everyone who is a part of an educational ecosystem, especially those who work directly at these intersections.

Importance of Special Education Teachers of Color

To date, we do not have books that chronicle the lives of special education teachers at the intersections of race and disability. Special education teachers of color have a unique role to play in educational spaces. First, they work directly at the intersections of race and disability, alongside the

6 Racism and Ableism in the Classroom and Teacher Education

complex tensions held by these two intersecting, overlapping identity constructions. Additionally, many live at these intersections as multiply marginalized disabled teachers of color. While special education teachers of color have the potential to be advocates for multiply marginalized disabled students of color and agents of change and resistance to the intersections of racism and ableism in schools, they are often absorbed into an ableist, racist, behaviorist system of special education teacher preparation in the United States (Kulkarni et al., 2022b). Narratives surrounding special education teachers of color in the public sphere tend to focus heavily on retention and attrition (Bettini et al., 2020) rather than some of the more systemic challenges they will inevitably face in schools.

Stories of the teacher shortages are often limited by placing the locus of control on teacher education programs when remedying teacher vacancies must also grapple with systemic racism, sociocultural views of teaching, structural supports such as pay and workload, and the kinds of teachers produced by programs reckoning with low enrollments and increased performance expectation requirements. Earlier this summer, teacher librarian Selena Carrion's tweet went viral describing the teacher shortage as "manufactured." She writes instead of the "intentional shortage of resources, pay, infrastructure, time, and support" (Carrion, 2022).

Billingsley and Bettini (2019) draw similar parallels for special education teacher retention and attrition. They note that working conditions such as the demands of the job, paperwork, supportive administrators and colleagues, resources, and appropriate compensation were all high factors in the turnover of special education teachers. Additionally, rather than focusing on the vacancies and teacher shortages in special education, I argue that teacher preparation programs need to think carefully about the kinds of teachers our programs produce. We want teachers who come in with racial and disability literacy, ideally, or at least an openness to deeply learning about these identity constructions in order to work to actively resist and dismantle systems of racism and ableism.

Book Overview

This book begins with the idea that we want critical special education teachers of color who disrupt racism and ableism in the classroom. I have been fortunate in my work as a special education teacher educator and researcher interviewing and working qualitatively with teachers of color these past six to seven years to have come across several incredible educators whose passions lie directly on centering the identities of their multiply marginalized disabled students. Many of them do this despite the challenges of ongoing neoliberal school reforms and difficult working conditions. I am grateful to be able to participate alongside them in the sharing of their narratives, not only to elevate their positioning as special education teachers of color but also to illustrate the immensely challenging systems under which they are expected to continue working. Yet another example of the intersections of racism and ableism is the expectation that special education teachers of color will work harder, longer, and without adequate compensation for their time and extensive efforts. While we, as teacher educators, must increase the number of special education teachers of color with critical understandings of racism and ableism in schools, we must also work collectively to dismantle the systems that perpetuate harm and "spirit murder" (Love, 2019) these teachers of multiply marginalized disabled students of color.

This book presents five critical case narratives of special education teachers of color spanning preschool through high school. Narratives are co-generated by each special education teacher of color with my support for analysis. Where possible, I avoid telling their story and allow them to share their experiences themselves. Each story is a combination of co-writing and expands upon earlier narratives each has shared qualitatively for research. Each teacher's unique, individual approaches to countering racism and ableism are described through their own words and their shared examples of practices. Collectively, there are also important ways in which their practices are connected. At their core, each of these teachers is deeply committed to continue unlearning of racism and ableism. Through their individual and collective efforts, each teacher is also committed to dismantling systems of oppression that impact multiply marginalized disabled students of color. Lastly, and perhaps most importantly, each teacher believes in collective student joy and helping their students build pride in their identities as students of color and as disabled. This effort is to actively shift away from narratives of disability as deficit, a source of pity, and the ongoing sorrow associated with being a student of color with disabilities. Zora Neale Hurston (1928) wrote in her piece *How It Feels to Be Colored Me*, "sometimes, I feel discriminated against, but it does not make me angry. It merely astonishes me. How can any deny themselves the pleasure of my company? It's beyond me." Therefore, this book is a celebration of these five special education teachers of color.

I sandwich the five narratives between contextual information about the state of California and the state of special education teachers of color (Chapter 1) and some of the more practical ways to integrate curriculum that highlights the full integration of race and disability in teacher education (Chapter 7). I include curriculum mapping work that connects critical

8 Racism and Ableism in the Classroom and Teacher Education

resources from disabled activists of color and those scholars sitting at the tensions of race and disability to the seven tenets of DisCrit (Annamma et al., 2013). I also introduce resources that draw from a new framework that marries DisCrit and Culturally Sustaining Pedagogies (Alim & Paris, 2017): Disability Centered Culturally Sustaining Pedagogies (Kulkarni et al., 2023). I conclude with some key examples of how the five teacher narratives enact resistance and cultivate joyful classrooms for multiply marginalized disabled children and youth (Chapter 8). Thus, this book utilizes and elevates the narratives of special education teachers of color, an overlooked and underserved population (Kulkarni, 2022b) as a vehicle for leaning into the tensions of race and disability.

As a final note, the majority of this book was written a couple of years before the 2024 presidential election. However, I must address some of the significant ramifications of that election on special education and diversity, equity, and inclusion (DEI). On March 20th, 2025, Donald J. Trump signed an executive order to close the Department of Education (EPI, 2025). The order has implications for the Individuals with Disabilities Education Act (IDEA) and furthers a right-wing agenda to eliminate free and appropriate public education (FAPE) for children with disabilities. In this book, I often refer to how we must resist current educational systems, which are fraught with ableism and racism. Though this book discusses dismantling such systems, it is not equivalent to the current executive order, which seeks to undermine and destroy educational opportunities. When I speak of dismantling ableist and racist systems, I am referring to ways that these systems can serve more students, particularly multiply marginalized disabled students, more equitably. The current administration in 2025 is not interested in equitably serving all students but in creating barriers to access for those who are often the most marginalized. I hope that this book, and the voices of special education teachers of color contained within it, will begin a more critical discussion about dismantling inequitable systems to eliminate barriers rather than create them.

Note

1 Henceforth, I refer to students of color with disabilities and multiply marginalized children/youth with disabilities or disabled youth as "multiply marginalized disabled students of color" to highlight the ways in which students are positioned by school systems. Person-first and identity-first language are used interchangeably depending on the types of scholarship that I summarize. In the co-written narratives, teachers may use their own terms (e.g., Black and Brown students with disabilities) to highlight the specific groups of students whom they work with.

References

Alim, H. S., & Paris, D. (2017). What is culturally sustaining pedagogy and why does it matter. *Culturally Sustaining Pedagogies: Teaching and Learning for Justice in a Changing World, 1*(24), 85–101.

Annamma, S., and Morrison, D. (2018). DisCrit classroom ecology: Using praxis to dismantle dysfunctional education ecologies. *Teaching and Teacher Education, 73*, 70–80. https://doi.org/10.1016/j.tate.2018.03.008

Annamma, S. A. (2017). *The pedagogy of pathologization: Dis/abled girls of color in the school-prison nexus*. Routledge.

Annamma, S. A., Connor, D., & Ferri, B. (2013). Dis/ability critical race studies (DisCrit): Theorizing at the intersections of race and dis/ability. *Race Ethnicity and Education, 16*(1), 1–31. https://doi.org/10.1080/13613324.2012.730511

Artiles, A. J. (2011). Toward an interdisciplinary understanding of educational equity and difference: The case of the racialization of ability. *Educational Researcher, 40*(9), 431–445. https://doi.org/10.3102/0013189X11429391

Artiles, A. J. (2013). Untangling the racialization of disabilities: An intersectionality critique across disability models. *Du Bois Review: Social Science Research on Race, 10*(2), 329–347. https://doi.org/10.1017/S1742058X13000271

Artiles, A. J. (2022). Interdisciplinary notes on the dual nature of disability: Disrupting ideology–ontology circuits in racial disparities research. *Literacy Research: Theory, Method, and Practice*. https://doi.org/10.1177/23813377221120106

Bell, C. (2010). Is disability studies actually white disability studies? *The Disability Studies Reader, 5*, 402–410.

Bettini, E., Gilmour, A. F., Williams, T. O., & Billingsley, B. (2020). Predicting special and general educators' intent to continue teaching using conservation of resources theory. *Exceptional Children, 86*(3), 310–329.

Billingsley, B., & Bettini, E. (2019). Special education teacher attrition and retention: A review of the literature. *Review of Educational Research, 89*(5), 697–744. https://doi.org/10.3102/00346543198624

Boda, P. A., Nusbaum, E. A., & Kulkarni, S. S. (2022). From 'what is' toward 'what if' through intersectionality: Problematizing ableist erasures and coloniality in racially just research. *International Journal of Research & Method in Education*, 1–14. https://doi.org/10.1080/1743727X.2022.2054981

Carrion, S. (2022, August 8). *The "teacher shortage" is manufactured. It's the result of an intentional shortage of everything else in education (and beyond): Proper pay, resources, respect, infrastructure, services, time, and ultimately care for children & the adults supporting them* [Tweet]. https://twitter.com/SelenaCarrion/status/1556794988972982275

Chatterjee, D. (2018). Interdependence is an ableist myth: Unlocking the power of community and healing. *The Body is Not an Apology*. https://thebodyisnotanapology.com/magazine/independence-is-an-ableist-myth-unlocking-the-power-of-community-in-healing/

Cioè-Peña, M. (2021). *(M)othering labeled children: Bilingualism and disability in the lives of Latinx mothers* (Vol. 131). Multilingual Matters.

Connor, D. J. (2008). *Urban narratives: Portraits in progress, life at the intersections of learning disability, race, & social class* (Vol. 5). Peter Lang.

Economic Policy Institute. (2025, March 21). *Executive order closing the Department of Education*. https://www.epi.org/policywatch/executive-order-on-closing-parts-of-the-department-of-education/

Erevelles, N. (2014). 'Crippin' Jim Crow: Disability, dis-location, and the school-to prison pipeline. In L. Ben-Moshe, C. Chapman, & A. C. Carey (Eds.), *Disability incarcerated: Imprisonment and disability in the United States and Canada* (pp. 81–99). Palgrave Macmillan. https://doi.org/10.1057/9781137388476_5

Farley, R., & Taeuber, A. F. (1974). Racial segregation in the public schools. *American Journal of Sociology, 79*(4), 888–905. https://doi.org/10.1086/225631

Harry, B., & Klingner, J. (2014). *Why are so many minority students in special education?* Teachers College Press.

Hurston, Z. N. (1928). *How it feels to be colored me*. Open Road Media.

Invalid, S. (2017). Skin, tooth, and bone – the basis of movement is our people: A disability justice primer. https://doi.org/10.1080/09688080.2017.1335999

Klingner, J. K., & Edwards, P. A. (2006). Cultural considerations with response to intervention models. *Reading Research Quarterly, 41*(1), 108–117. https://doi.org/10.1598/RRQ.41.1.6

Kulkarni, S. S. (2015). *Beliefs about disability, race, and culture of urban special education teachers and their retention decisions* [Doctoral Dissertation, The University of Wisconsin-Madison].

Kulkarni, S. S. (2022a). Navigating South Asian/Desi identity as a teacher educator in Silicon Valley. In A. R. Mysore (Eds.), *Narratives of South Asian social justice educators in North America*. Lexington Books.

Kulkarni, S. S. (2022b). Special education teachers of color and their beliefs about dis/ability and race: Counter-stories of smartness and goodness. *Curriculum Inquiry, 51*(5), 496–521. https://doi.org/10.1080/03626784.2021.1938973

Kulkarni, S. S., & Hanley-Maxwell, C. (2015). Preservice teachers' student teaching experiences in East Africa. *Teacher Education Quarterly, 42*(4), 59–81. https://www.jstor.org/stable/teaceducquar.42.4.59

Kulkarni, S. S., & Parmar, J. (2017). Culturally and linguistically diverse student and family perspectives of AAC. *Augmentative and Alternative Communication, 33*(3), 170–180. https://doi.org/10.1080/07434618.2017.1346706

Kulkarni, S. S., Miller, A. L., Nusbaum, E. A., Pearson, H., & Brown, L. X. Z. (2023). Toward disability-centered culturally sustaining pedagogies in teacher education. *Critical Studies in Education, 65*, 107–127.

Kulkarni, S. S., Nusbaum, E., & Boda, P. (2021). DisCrit at the margins of teacher education: Informing curriculum, visibilization, and disciplinary integration. *Race Ethnicity and Education, 24*(5), 654–670. https://doi.org/10.1080/1361 3324.2021.1918404

Love, B. L. (2019). *We want to do more than survive: Abolitionist teaching and the pursuit of educational freedom*. Beacon Press.

Love, H. R., & Beneke, M. R. (2021). Pursuing justice-driven inclusive education research: Disability critical race theory (DisCrit) in early childhood. *Topics in Early Childhood Special Education, 41*(1), 31–44. https://doi.org/10.1177/0271121421990833

Migliarini, V., & Annamma, S. A. (2020). Classroom and behavior management: (Re) conceptualization through disability critical race theory. In *Handbook on promoting social justice in education* (pp. 1511–1532). https://doi.org/10.100 7/978-3-030-14625-2_95

Miller, A. L. (2020). Disabled girls of color excavate exclusionary literacy practices and generate promising sociospatial-textual solutions. *International Journal of Qualitative Studies in Education*, 1–24. https://doi.org/10.1080/09518398.202 0.1828649

Nusbaum, E. A., & Steinborn, M. L. (2019). A "visibilizing" project: "Seeing" the ontological erasure of disability in teacher education and social studies curricula. *Journal of Curriculum Theorizing, 34*(1).

Patel, L. (2019). Fugitive practices: Learning in a settler colony. *Educational Studies, 55*(3), 253–261. https://doi.org/10.1080/00131946.2019.1605368

Pugach, M. C., Matewos, A. M., & Gomez-Najarro, J. (2021). Disability and the meaning of social justice in teacher education research: A precarious guest at the table? *Journal of Teacher Education, 72*(2), 237–250.

Sauer, J. S., & Rossetti, Z. (2019). *Affirming disability: Strengths-based portraits of culturally diverse families*. Teachers College Press.

SJSU History. (n.d.). https://www.sjsu.edu/about/history/timeline.php

Waitoller, F. R., & Thorius, K. K. (Eds.). (2022). *Sustaining disabled youth: Centering disability in asset pedagogies*. Teachers College Press.

Walker, V. S. (2018). *The lost education of Horace Tate: Uncovering the hidden heroes who fought for justice in schools*. The New Press.

Will, M., & Mitchell, C. (2019, September 9). The push to get more teachers of color in special education classrooms. *Education Week*. https://www.edweek.org/teaching-learning/the-push-to-get-more-teachers-of-color-in-special-education-classrooms/2019/09

Wong, A. (Ed.). (2020). *Disability visibility: First-person stories from the twenty-first century*. Vintage.

1

UNDERSTANDING RACISM AND ABLEISM IN TEACHER EDUCATION THROUGH SPECIAL EDUCATION TEACHERS OF COLOR

As a first-year special education teacher in Oakland, California, I was fortunate to learn about a fellowship through the University of San Francisco called Teacher Education Advancement for a Multicultural Society (TEAMS/AmeriCorps). The TEAMS/AmeriCorps program provided Saturday seminars for teachers around issues of equity, diversity, and social justice. We heard from critical voices in the field, such as Jeffrey Duncan Andrade and Geneva Gay, and read poetry, such as "We Real Cool" by Gwendolyn Brooks. Program mentors also supported new teachers in developing service-learning opportunities for our students. The program was invaluable in helping me to address issues of racial and social justice in my classroom. Unfortunately, however, as in many social justice spaces, disability was the "uninvited guest at the table" (Connor, 2012). While the program included a few special education doctoral candidates as mentors, none had experience supporting students with complex needs, which, at the time, included all of the students in my classroom.

During that year, I dedicated my service-learning project to environmental justice. My students learned the basics of recycling, and we worked to create a program for the middle school that would collect bottles and cans from each classroom and deposit them at the local recycling center. Although it seemed like a small task, this project provided students with leadership opportunities, exposure in a school where they were heavily segregated to my classroom in a portable at the back of the school, and direct connections to science, math, and community living Individualized Education Program (IEP) goals.

DOI: 10.4324/9781003653783-2

If I were to do it again, I would have probably added opportunities for students to present their learning across this unit to the school, creating more opportunities for them to be rendered visible. I might have also looked into partnerships with local environmental agencies. Despite the minute scale of the project, however, it began my thinking about the tensions of social justice and the inclusion of disability as a social marker. Unfortunately, neither special education nor social justice education really addresses disability as an identity rather than a deficit.

Brantlinger (2006) notes how the field of special education emphasizes a need for individuals with disabilities to be fixed both through the perspective of viewing disability as needing a cure and how racist and ableist identities are ascribed to individual students. Bornstein et al. (2023) note how special education stems from "racist imperatives" (p. 3). Kafka (2011) also traces the origins of special education to the compliance and cultural remediation of multiply marginalized youth, emphasizing how behavior must conform to White, nondisabled norms in schools. Such attitudes have led to ongoing challenges with disproportionate representation of students of color in special education and an overwhelming number of multiply marginalized youth in segregated settings (Skiba & Rausch, 2013). It has also, I argue, contributed to a field based on the majority perspectives of white women teachers.

Inherently, special education and teacher education programs located within institutions of higher education are steeped in whiteness, racism, and ableism. Like the "old boys club" culture of executive boardrooms, membership in special education teacher circles follows a similar principle of "closure" or "the idea that social groups restrict access to opportunity on the basis of shared traits and experiences" (Michelman et al., 2022, p. 846). In the case of special education teachers, this club is made up of white women. The field is so predominantly made up of this population, in fact, that research that specifically attended to special education teachers of color did not really begin until 2018.

Teachers of Color

Early studies incorporating special education teachers of color often fell under the guise of broader conversations regarding teachers of color and interests in diversifying the special education teaching workforce. I begin by describing the early research in these two areas, followed by a description of the California context of special education and credentialing, and then provide an overview of the frameworks and narratives that guide this book.

14 Racism and Ableism in the Classroom and Teacher Education

Recruitment and Education of Teachers of Color

Recent federal data notes how Black, Indigenous, People of Color (BIPOC) populations include 37% of adults and 50% of children nationwide (NCES, 2019). Unfortunately, however, just 19% of the educator workforce includes BIPOC teachers. From a lens of understanding the research evidence that illustrates the direct impact of teachers of color on students of color, Gist and Bristol (2022) note several key areas of research on teachers of color such as: Recruitment, Retention, MSIs, Human Resource Development and Induction, Mentorship, and Intersectionality.

According to Villegas et al. (2012), efforts to diversify the teaching workforce gained traction around the 1980s when data began to reveal the ethnoracial backgrounds of teachers. By the 1990s, there were recruitment strategies that included high school pipeline programs, community college partnerships, and career programs and grants to support paraprofessionals in becoming teachers. More recently, recruitment has focused on Grow Your Own programs, supporting and engaging teachers along the continuum of becoming a teacher (Gist et al., 2019).

Carver-Thomas et al. (2022) note how recruiting teachers of color using alternative or fast-track programs can actually exacerbate attrition among this population. Instead, the authors suggest that retention is linked with high-quality preparation and several key strategies, such as supportive pathways into teaching, comprehensive induction programs, and improved working conditions. Retaining teachers begins with access to strong teacher preparation that provides support such as loan forgiveness programs, scholarships, residencies, course articulation opportunities such as combination licensure and master's programs or credits for partial work in community colleges, adjustments to licensure and testing requirements, and incentive programs for high-performing programs. Additionally, providing strong mentorship programs such as being matched with an experienced mentor or participating in useful seminars and professional learning experiences. Lastly, it is important to include stronger preparation for leadership, which impacts school climate and working conditions for teachers of color.

Historically, the preparation of teachers of color has predominantly come from institutions that are defined as MSIs. Under Title III of the Higher Education Act of 1965, MSIs include Historically Black Colleges (HBCUs), Predominantly Black Institutions (PBIs), Hispanic-Serving Institutions (HSIs), Tribal Colleges or Universities (TCUs), Native American Non-Tribal Institutions (NANTIs), Alaskan Native or Native Hawaiian-Serving Institutions (ANNHIs), and Asian American and Native American Pacific Islander-Serving Institutions (AANAPISIs). Unlike predominantly white institutions, MSIs are considered "nurturing citadels" for students of color (Fenwick & Akua, 2022, p. 237). Teacher candidates of color attending MSIs tend to participate in a knowledge transfer process whereby they learn from larger numbers of faculty of color and pass this knowledge on to their P-12 students of color.

Another area that greatly impacts teachers of color and their retention and support is the role of human resources. In a policy brief conducted by the Regional Educational Laboratory of Education Northwest (Greenberg et al., 2019), the authors note the importance of human resources and induction in building a teacher of color workforce. Specific suggestions for recruitment, hiring, and onboarding teachers of color included building institutional partnerships, extended outreach programs involving teachers of color in their own hiring process, working to create strategic placements, and building capacity to support teachers of color (Fenwick & Akua, 2022).

Supporting teachers of color and retaining them must also include strong mentorship. Mentorship enhances professionalization and creates opportunities for capacity building. Morales et al. (2022) found that teachers of color viewed more formal mentorship as transactional, while more informal mentorship was viewed as authentic care. The authors call for mentorship to move away from using the same tools that have often been used with dominant groups with teachers of color and emphasize the use of critical mentorship.

The above areas highlighted key areas of research consideration for teachers of color. As an area of emerging research, intersectionality aims to highlight how ethnoracial diversity intersects with other identity markers such as disability, gender, and sexuality (Kulkarni et al., 2024). Research in this area on teachers of color aims to highlight both intersectional identities of teachers of color, including those that identify as queer or disabled, for example, and to describe how teachers of color may address the multiply marginalized identities of their students in schools.

Special Education Teachers of Color

In July 2002, the President's Commission on Special Education published the report *A New Era: Revitalizing Special Education for Children and Their Families* which highlighted a shortage of qualified special education teachers and a need to recruit and retain special education teachers representing the diversity of children in the classroom (Berdine, 2003). Specifically, among its findings, the report emphasized a need for students with disabilities to have highly qualified special education teachers. The report

16 Racism and Ableism in the Classroom and Teacher Education

built momentum for future research and shifts in special education practices that advocated for a diverse special education workforce.

Early Research on a Diverse Special Education Workforce

Deborah Voltz, in her early piece in the 1990s, set a stage for what later became articles advocating for a diverse workforce in special education. In Voltz (1998), for example, her editorial exchange began an important conversation in the Journal of Teacher Education and Special Education that moved from how teachers are prepared to meet the demands of a culturally and linguistically diverse student population to the need to increase diversity in the special education teaching workforce. However, one of the earliest pieces to advocate directly for a culturally and linguistically diverse teaching workforce in special education, Tyler et al. (2004) showcased the national concern over recruiting and retaining special education teachers from culturally and linguistically diverse backgrounds and provided a series of important themes in the successful preparation of diverse special education teachers, including recruitment, retention, alternative certification, and post-teaching preparation. The authors suggested that diverse candidates could be recruited using word of mouth, targeted media campaigns, through existing candidates from diverse backgrounds, and by showcasing successful candidates. They suggested that retention includes strategies such as providing targeted academic support, providing grants or other funding opportunities, cultural sensitivity support within teacher training programs, and mentorship through diverse faculty.

Billingsley's (2005) book on retaining special education teachers also briefly touches on the importance of recruiting and retaining culturally and linguistically diverse special education teachers. Citing the earlier work of Tyler et al. (2004), she notes a short supply of culturally and linguistically diverse special educators and the implications of diversifying the field for inappropriate referrals, academic achievement gaps between diverse students and white students, and improved multicultural communication (Billingsley, 2005). Shortly after, Thornton et al. (2007) advocated for systemic reform of job-level satisfaction of special education teachers in order to reduce teacher shortages. They argued that if policymakers and leaders were going to meet the educational needs of students with disabilities, there must be an investment in cultural and linguistic diversity.

These early works paved the way for other work that looked at special education teacher attrition, retention, and recruitment. For example, Skiba et al. (2006) noted through interviews with teachers how referral rates for students with disabilities were much higher among white women teachers than almost any other racial group. While we know that white women make up the majority of the special education teacher workforce, the authors still found proportionally higher referral rates among white women teachers. Though much of the early work made early inferences to the need for special education teachers of color, it took nearly 10 years before this specific body of literature emerged.

Trainor et al. (2019) also generated a special issue focusing on the racial/ethnic diversity of special education teachers. The authors noted the importance of students having access to special education teachers of color or teachers who form a racial/ethnic and cultural match to their backgrounds. In focusing on equity, the special issue engaged a conversation about special education teacher diversity, access of racially and ethnically diverse special education teachers to the profession, and an overall cultural match between students and their teachers.

Early conversations about retention and "cultural sensitivity" support within an existing teacher education program (Tyler et al., 2004), without examining how programs perpetuate practices that marginalize or exclude special education candidates of color, gloss over systemic issues including how teacher preparation programs engage in performing whiteness and are inherently ableist in the demands and expectations of future teachers. For example, Bornstein et al. (2023) shared that there may be calls for reducing disproportionality in special education through culturally responsive instruction and interventions without specifically attending to the structures and systems that generate these ongoing inequities. In special education teacher education, standards and requirements are often structured around directed instruction and interventions meant to aid students with disabilities in appearing more developmentally and behaviorally nondisabled, and special education teachers who question such practices are thought to be noncompliant or difficult. Preparation programs increasingly also place unrealistic expectations and demands on special education teachers, such as high credit loads, expensive testing fees, and consequential performance assessments. Such demands leave very little room for disability accommodations.

Second, specifically pairing special education teachers of color with mentors or faculty of color often places undue burden on these faculty members. It is known that faculty of color in higher education often take on additional responsibilities and mentorship roles with respect to students of color (Domingo et al., 2022), often performing more university service at the expense of research that weighs heavily in tenure and promotion decisions. Additionally, simply assigning a mentor of color does not always support the critical growth and development of special education teachers if programmatic structures remain racist and ableist. Simply assigning special education teachers of color to faculty of color also does not solve the larger systemic issues plaguing teacher education spaces.

Overall, early authors dedicated to reducing teacher shortages and attrition focused heavily on the need for a more diverse workforce. While Tyler et al. (2004) drew direct attention to the lack of a diverse special education teacher workforce, Billingsley (2005) and Thornton et al. (2007) shortly followed with an emphasis on policies and practices to recruit and retain diverse special education teachers. Early strategies by these scholars focused heavily on solutions that would simply bring more special education teachers of color into the classroom, suggesting pipeline recruitment efforts and mentorship support. Though these efforts are not at odds with the current research on teachers of color (see Gist & Bristol, 2022), much of this early work focused on supply at the expense of structural and systemic changes.

Recent Research on Culturally Sustaining Special Education Teacher Education

In order to create shifts and broader changes in schools, there has been a focus on integrating culturally sustaining pedagogies as a framework in teacher education. While much of this work is focused on highlighting the experiences of multiply marginalized disabled students of color, the role of disability is largely absent (González et al., 2024). More recent attention, however, has focused on efforts to integrate culturally sustaining pedagogies into special education. These efforts include program redesign efforts (Barrio, 2021), single-course approaches (Santamaría-Graff et al., 2020), fieldwork opportunities (Kulkarni & Hanley-Maxwell, 2015; Santamaría-Graff et al., 2009) and in-service efforts such as professional learning communities (Moore, 2018) and affinity groups (Kulkarni et al., 2022). Across each of these domains, the role of special education teachers of color remains a critical connection that draws directly from the experiences of multiply marginalized teachers.

Recent Research and the Experiences of Special Education Teachers of Color

Only recently has research on special education teachers of color moved toward the experiences of teachers in classrooms and preparation programs. One of the earliest pieces highlighting the lack of research on the experiences of special education teachers of color was a commentary written by Scott (2016), which began a line of research on Black, male special education teachers. Scott (2016) argued that given the overrepresentation of Black, male students in special education programs, there is limited engagement with Black, male special educators. His paper highlighted needs and priorities that parallel those found in the recent *Handbook of Research on Teachers of Color and Indigenous Teachers* (Gist & Bristol, 2022), such as extensive funding and compensation for special education teachers of color, innovative, and alternative programming, and ways to invest in teachers in the early parts of their careers. Scott and Alexander (2019) went on to interview 18 Black, male special education teachers about their retention and recruitment experiences and suggested strategies for increasing the special education teacher of color workforce and retaining existing Black, male teachers. Scott (2019) also interviewed Black, male special education teachers to understand their rationales for choosing alternatively certified programming. Like Tyler et al. (2004), the author noted how mentorship from Black faculty members in their teacher licensure program provided critical support that encouraged these teachers to choose alternative licensure.

In 2021, Cormier and Scott looked at a broader sample of minoritized special education teachers and provided some strategies and supports to encourage teachers' personal belongingness and their role as individuals advocating for both racial and disability justice. In 2021, I also published a piece that chronicled narrative reflections and interviews with special education teachers of color using a lens of smartness and goodness (Kulkarni, 2021). Data from this study came from a 2018 sample of special education teachers of color working in local Southern California school districts. When I worked as a faculty member in an HSI in Southern California, I worked with a majority of teachers of color, yet the curriculum being provided to these teachers was heavily watered down and included no personal perspectives from disabled people and/or people of color. I spent three years working to shift the curriculum of these courses using DisCrit (Annamma et al., 2013) as a guide. What emerged was a subset of teachers committed to racial justice and anti-ableist practices for students with disabilities.

Building on this work (Kulkarni et al., 2022), I began working with a broader group of special education teachers of color, whom I coined "SETOC." Reflecting on the challenges of participants in the 2021 study, I began to notice similar patterns of stress and isolation faced by teacher candidates working in the Bay Area. Therefore, I worked with two graduate students, both of whom also identified as SETOC, to develop a critical affinity group. We collected data on how the affinity space helped bring much-needed support to SETOC engaged in anti-racist and anti-ableist education. The group met biweekly over the course of the pandemic using Zoom. Topics included navigating general education spaces, being the only

20 Racism and Ableism in the Classroom and Teacher Education

teacher of color, and finding ways to resist racist and ableist school systems. Through the study, we coined the term "disability battle fatigue" to highlight the challenges experienced by special education teachers of color advocating for anti-ableist and anti-racist changes, only to be met with resistance by teachers and leaders.

Siuty and Atwood (2022) also shared the qualitative case of Sarah, a Black special education teacher, to generate resistance. Using DisCrit classroom ecologies (Annamma et al., 2018a) as a framework, the authors showed how Sarah enacted transformative practices of resistance to deficit framings of students with disabilities and students of color in her school. For example, Sarah challenged her colleagues who believed that her program for students with disabilities was not academically rigorous and meaningful and pushed back against any authority that emphasized compliance over social-emotional learning.

Since my dissertation in 2015, much of my work has chronicled some of the immediate and systemic challenges faced by SETOC in California. It is important to understand, therefore, how the process of teacher education works in the state and how the teacher education program and licensure and standards requirements might contribute to retention and attrition for SETOC. Below, I provide information about the California-specific teacher education and special education context, history, and credentialing process, and how this resembles and differs from the national context. Additionally, I discuss the existing research on teachers of color and limited but emerging research on special education teachers of color. I end this chapter with an argument for the stories of special education teachers of color, which have not been shared broadly in the special education research and research of teachers of color.

Teacher Education and Special Education in the California Context

Teaching in the California context is challenging. In 1998, Brunetti noted an increasingly diverse student population, especially across languages, and a shortage of highly qualified teachers as huge issues impacting the state. Often one of the reasons that scholars and policymakers view student demographic diversity as a deficit is that special education teachers are predominantly, as noted above, a club of white women. In order for diversity to be viewed through the lens of an asset rather than a deficit across student demographics, the teacher workforce needs to reflect the student population, and/or teachers need to have the self-efficacy to embrace student differences.

California is both unique and similar to other states across the United States. Like most other large states, including Texas and New York, California's racialized minority population of students has surpassed its white student population (Cooc & Yang, 2016; Scott et al., 2023). Also, like other large states, special education teachers of color lag behind general education teachers, with only around 22% of teachers identifying as teachers of color. Even less data is known about special education teachers of color with disabilities, which highlights the importance of this book, one that contains example chapters from special education teachers of color who do identify as disabled.

Unique to California, however, is that despite a recent investment in high-quality preparation programs and an overall preparation satisfaction rating of candidates, including those from diverse demographic backgrounds, over 50% of diverse candidates, including special education candidates, do not have access to some form of student teaching (Kemper & Arturo, 2022). Additionally, a recent report from the San Francisco civil grand jury found that in the San Francisco Unified School District (SFUSD), nearly 25% of teachers are not fully credentialed (Echevarria, 2023). Across the state, that figure is around 20% of teachers working on permits or waivers and is attributed to statewide shortages in fields such as math, science, and special education (NCES, 2019). However, California's new teacher education standards have shifted their focus toward higher-order thinking skills, socio-emotional learning, and supporting teachers of emergent bilingual students (Kemper & Arturo, 2022).

Special Education Credentialing Process

California includes three primary pathways toward teacher certification: (1) completing a pre-service teacher preparation program with a supervised student teaching component prior to serving as a teacher of record in a classroom; (2) serving as an intern candidate who has demonstrated subject matter competency via a California Subject Examination for Teachers (CSET) test or coursework equivalency and serving as a teacher of record while completing their credential; or (3) entering the profession on an emergency-style permit when there is an unfilled vacancy while subsequently enrolling in a credential program. The credential authorized for teaching students with disabilities is called an education specialist credential and authorizes the candidate to teach across grade levels.

A caveat to this is that special education operates across several focus strands: early childhood, mild to moderate disabilities, extensive support needs, deaf and hard of hearing, visual impairments, and physical/health

22 Racism and Ableism in the Classroom and Teacher Education

impairments. Teachers working in the first strand may only work with students from birth to five. California recently also adopted a transitional kindergarten model, which requires its own set of supplemental requirements. For special education credentials in California, teachers can earn a preliminary credential valid for up to five years and a clear credential that is valid for life. Special education teachers can practice as teachers of record within the following types of settings:

- General education classrooms: teaching alongside general education teachers in classrooms where students with or without disabilities learn together.
- Resource classrooms: teaching small groups or individual students either through a push-in model, where students receive intervention support within a general education classroom, or in a separate space away from the general education classroom.
- Special Day classrooms: in California, special day classes are classrooms that only include students with disabilities. These may be grouped by category (i.e., Mild/Moderate; Extensive Support Needs).
- Specialized schools: schools that include special education services in a segregated school for students with disabilities.
- Correctional facilities: facilities for students with disabilities who may have also had trouble with the law.
- Home/Hospital settings: for students with disabilities who may require intensive medical care or support.
- Nonpublic school settings: these include other nonpublic school settings that do not fall under the correctional facilities.

Data on Special Education Teachers of Color From California

Cooc and Yang's (2016) study highlighted the trends of special education teacher credentials in California from 1997 until 2014. Though the number of special education teachers of color continues to lag behind the number of white special education teachers in the state, the authors show that there is rapid growth in the number of special education teachers of color in the state. In plotting the growth of special education teachers of color, the authors find an over 135% increase compared to teachers of color without special education credentials. Overall, though the percentage of special education teachers of color across the state for the data period was only 29%, the authors share a rapid growth of teachers of color in special education and a decrease in white students with disabilities in public schools across the state (Cooc & Yang, 2016). This emphasizes the importance of special education teacher education that works to decenter whiteness and ableism and provides much-needed critical support for special education teachers of color across the state.

Scott et al.'s (2023) critical quantitative analysis of the retention decisions of special education teachers of color also sampled the largest number of participants from California (127 of 778 respondents). This suggests that California has a larger sample of special education teachers of color and may also have a larger number of classrooms with students of color with disabilities. Though the data on special education teachers of color are not extensive across the state, it is important to note that California is a leader among states representing special education teachers of color, which has potential implications for preparation across other states.

As Fenwick and Akua (2022) noted earlier, the role of MSIs may also contribute to the larger numbers of teachers of color across the state. California has the largest public university system in the United States: The California State University System. As mentioned earlier, this system includes 23 institutions across the state, all of which are designated MSIs. Given the level of preparation of teachers of color across the MSIs in California, it is not hard to imagine why the state would be at the forefront of special education preparation for teachers of color.

DisCrit Framework

Despite being one of the leading states for the number of special education teachers of color, California, like other states across the United States, has a mixture of teacher preparation programs that vary in quality and content. In my earlier work on special education teachers of color (Kulkarni, 2021), I highlight how preparation programs for special education are often steeped in whiteness and ableism and how I worked as a teacher educator in an MSI to undo these practices by utilizing the framework Disability Studies Critical Race Theory (DisCrit; Annamma et al., 2013). Beneke and Love (2022), for example, emphasize how technocratic aspects of schooling, particularly for young children, uphold notions of whiteness and ableism by holding children to universal developmental milestones and standards and erasing the knowledge of multiply marginalized youth and families. In other words, special education, even at the early childhood stage, expects that children, especially children of color with disabilities, meet milestones around play, speech, self-care, and behavior that are based on White, English-speaking, Westernized cultural norms.

We can see similar parallels with special education teachers similarly being held to universal standards of teaching quality, such as emphasizing directed instruction *for* students with disabilities and their families, rather than *with*. Additionally, preparation programs leave little room for the valuable experiences of special education teachers of color. For example, in Kulkarni et al. (2022) we noted how SETOC all had difficult and sometimes confrontational experiences with white women at their school sites, yet there was never an opportunity for them to share these experiences or seek support during their credential programs. Siuty et al. (2024) also shared how the dynamics of white-ability saviorism are especially prevalent in urban teacher preparation programs.

DisCrit, therefore, provides opportunities to examine how whiteness and ability uphold notions of normalcy in special education teacher education programs. Bornstein et al. (2023) note how Disability Studies Critical Race Theory (DisCrit; Annamma et al., 2013) asserts that special education is "a persistent example of benevolent racism" that focuses more on reducing impairment and controlling student behavior, especially for students of color, rather than challenging how systems multiply marginalize youth (p. 3). DisCrit proposes the following seven tenets: (1) racism and ableism circulate interdependently to uphold notions of normalcy; (2) values multidimensional identities and troubles singular notions of identity such as race or disability or class or gender or sexuality; (3) emphasizes the social construction of race and ability and recognizes the material and psychological impacts of being labeled as raced and/or disabled, which sets one outside of Western cultural norms; (4) privileges the voices of marginalized populations, traditionally not acknowledged within research; (5) considers the legal and historical implications of disability and race and how these have been used separately and together to deny the rights of some citizens; (6) recognizes Whiteness and ability as property and that gains for people with disabilities have largely been made based on the interest convergence of White, middle-class citizens; and (7) recognizes all forms of resistance and activism.

As a framework, DisCrit enables a deeper interrogation of race and ability in teacher education. Particularly for special education teachers of color, DisCrit allows for an examination of how teachers' experiences have included examples of racism and ableism as well as how they interrupt these multiple and intersecting oppressions in their P-12 classroom practices. We can also begin to understand how teacher preparation spaces replicate some of the same inequities seen in P-12 classrooms and can draw from multiply marginalized teachers of color and their experiences navigating special education teacher education.

Although my earlier work (Kulkarni, 2021) was informed by DisCrit and shared the narrative experiences of special education teachers of color as they navigated the frameworks of smartness and goodness, my later work (Kulkarni et al., 2022), which included direct engagements with SETOC as they shared their challenges in a critical affinity space and a book chapter on SETOC experiences as teachers of color and as disabled, provided more in-depth first-person views. Building on these first-person experiences and narratives is emerging work, but it is critical in decentering whiteness and ableism in special education teacher preparation and classrooms. In Chapter 7, I will introduce Disability-Centered Culturally Sustaining Pedagogies (DCCSPs; Kulkarni et al., 2023) as a framework that expands DisCrit by simultaneously engaging culturally sustaining pedagogies (Paris & Alim, 2017).

Narratives of Special Education Teachers of Color

From federal and state level expectations for teachers' performance to how individual universities structure and schedule coursework, teacher education programs were never designed to highlight the assets and gifts of multiply marginalized teachers such as teachers of color and/or disabled teachers. It is at this point that the following questions become critical:

(1) How does one continue to be a part of a system (in this case special education) when that system enacts harm upon multiply marginalized teachers, students, families, and communities (in this case multiply marginalized disabled people of color)?
(2) If one works outside of the system of special education, how might one still work to dismantle the system?

For special education teachers of color, these questions allude to the ongoing tensions of special education's existence for multiply marginalized disabled students of color, their families, and communities, as well as special education teachers of color committed to anti-racist and anti-ableist practices in schools. If, as the first question suggests, special education teachers of color remain within the system of special education, it is important to note the physical, psychological, and emotional labor they would need to endure to continue working toward changing the field, as was evidenced in our work on disability battle fatigue (Kulkarni et al., 2022). The stories of special education teachers of color shared in this book will highlight some of these tensions and the emotional/psychological work that special education teachers of color undergo in moving toward liberatory, anti-racist, and anti-ableist education.

As a woman of color with invisible disabilities, both of these questions highlight the challenges I personally face when negotiating my role as a special education teacher educator. One of the ways I continue to grapple with these tensions is to work closely with special education teacher candidates to decenter whiteness in all the spaces I occupy: as a course instructor, as a researcher, as a colleague, and as a collaborator. As a teacher educator of color, however, I have been fortunate to have developed relationships with a host of special education teachers of color, many of whom are having similar tensions with racism and ableism in their P-12 classrooms and in teacher education. Their continued persistence and resistance to teaching while multiply marginalized is what drives my passion to continue my work.

First-person narratives, especially those that highlight marginalized and multiply marginalized experiences, continue to be limited in special education. As Cioè-Peña (2018) notes in her work on Latinx mothers of children with disabilities, most narratives of families and schools are written without their voices and perspectives, thus generating a dominant framework for what school performance and family involvement should look like. From a methodological perspective, first-person narratives are often seen as less rigorous than large-sample studies where claims can be easily extrapolated across a broad population. The challenge is that many of these broader samples fail to capture the daily lived experiences of multiply marginalized peoples and identify the successes and challenges they face within the racist, ableist system of schooling. First-person narratives of special education teachers of color highlight the complexities of lived experiences of working at the intersections of disability and race (Kulkarni, 2021). For each special education teacher of color in this book, I look to the objective Ladson-Billings (2022) shared in *Dreamkeepers: Successful Teachers of African American Children* to "pull together the commonalities" of teachers' "philosophies, pedagogies, and personal commitments" (p. 32).

Organization of the Book

This book, and the joint narratives in each chapter, sits with the two challenging questions I pose above from the vantage point of special education teachers of color. All of these teachers have several years of experience working with multiply marginalized disabled students of color across the P-12 grade span in California. The special education teachers of color who share their stories in this book hold intersectional identities as special education teachers, as leaders, as BIPOC, and, for some, as disabled. The book represents the first opportunity for special education teachers of color to share these identities as they navigate P-12 public schools in California. Though they hold identities as special education teachers in a system that is racist, ableist, and heavily behaviorist, each of these teachers represents individuals who are working/have worked in direct resistance to multiple, intersecting oppressions in their schools.

In Chapter 2, we meet LaVeda, a Black preschool special education teacher who shares how her efforts to deeply reflect upon her young students as individuals with valuable thoughts, feelings, and opinions. LaVeda shares her journey as a Black, female growing up in Compton, California, and practices that encourage her to learn about and integrate her students' identities into her classroom. LaVeda and I share her story and how she reframes existing narratives of her students, most of whom identify as students of color with disabilities.

In Chapter 3, we meet Loriann, currently a Latina high school principal and formerly an elementary special education teacher in Oakland, California. Loriann chronicles a journey of being underestimated in schools and never wanting to go back into the classroom. After she returned, she worked to incorporate principles of restorative justice to help honor students' voices in designing instruction and classroom community. In Chapter 3, Loriann and I share her challenges with special education, her advice for special education teachers of color, and her critical practices to resist simplistic narratives surrounding her students and their behavior.

In Chapter 4, we meet Samuel, a Black, disabled former special education teacher who shares how he negotiated his identity as Black, as a person with a learning disability, and as a male special education teacher while working with his mostly Black and Brown middle school students.

In Chapter 5, we meet Joanna, a Latina special education teacher with health considerations who has experienced houselessness and trauma. Joanna chronicles her own struggles growing up and finding school to be a safe haven. She juxtaposes this with how her students, who identify as mostly male students of color with disabilities, are excluded as a form of discipline and how this exclusion leaves them feeling that school is not a place for them. She envisions a more inclusive space of resistance and abolitionist schooling where students' humanity is recognized and celebrated.

Lastly, in Chapter 6, we meet Ashley, a Black female special education teacher who works predominantly with high school and transition-aged students in and out of community settings. Although Ashley has had to challenge some of her own beliefs around disability and ableism and, as she notes, some of the challenges with this acknowledgment in the Black community, she also has become a fierce advocate for her students, especially in settings outside of the physical space of school.

Each of the teachers featured in this book has even gone beyond addressing racism and ableism in their schools to specifically center multiply marginalized disabled voices in the curriculum. At the end of the book, I will share a new framework—DCCSPs (Kulkarni et al., 2023)—and showcase how these teachers have moved to re-center their curriculum using disabled activists and scholars and their produced materials, such as books, poems, podcasts, and videos, to directly engage race and ability with their multiply marginalized students of color. Therefore, these teachers have moved from resistance to oppressive systems to embracing new materials and concepts with their students.

At the end of this book, I spend time highlighting why DCCSPs, which marry DisCrit and Culturally Sustaining Pedagogies (Paris & Alim, 2017), are important in unlearning ableism at any age (P-12). Particularly, DCCSPs support the direct knowledge provided by disabled community activists and disability justice advocates being integrated into a reimagined teacher education, one that acknowledges how important knowledge about disability and its intersections is not held solely in institutions of higher education, but with communities, particularly multiply marginalized disabled communities. I share how integrating such knowledge into special education teacher preparation spaces is so critical and how special education teachers of color can lead us in this endeavor.

References

Annamma, S., & Morrison, D. (2018a). DisCrit classroom ecology: Using praxis to dismantle dysfunctional education ecologies. *Teaching and Teacher Education*, 73, 70–80.

Annamma, S. A., Connor, D., & Ferri, B. (2013). Dis/ability critical race studies (DisCrit): Theorizing at the intersections of race and dis/ability. *Race Ethnicity and Education*, 16(1), 1–31.

Barrio, B. L. (2021). Understanding culturally responsive practices in teacher preparation: An avenue to address disproportionality in special education. *Teaching Education*, 32(4), 437–456. https://doi.org/10.1080/10476210.2020.1796956

Beneke, M. R., & Love, H. R. (2022). A DisCrit analysis of quality in early childhood: Toward pedagogies of wholeness, access, and interdependence. *Teachers College Record*, 124(12), 192–219.

Berdine, W. H. (2003). The President's commission on excellence in special education: Implications for the special education practitioner. *Preventing School Failure: Alternative Education for Children and Youth*, 47(2), 92–95.

Billingsley, B. S. (2005). *Cultivating and keeping committed special education teachers: What principals and district leaders can do*. Corwin Press.

Bornstein, J., Lustick, H., Shallish, L. V. H. L., & Okilwa, N. (2023). Seeing direct accountability for disproportionate discipline and dis/ability classification. *AERA Open*, 9(1), 1–14. https://doi.org/10.1177/23328584231206166

Brantlinger, E. A. (Ed.). (2006). *Who benefits from special education?: Remediating (fixing) other people's children*. Routledge.

Brunetti, G. J. (1998). Teacher education: A look at its future. *Teacher Education Quarterly*, 59–64.

Carver-Thomas, D., Hyler, M. E., & Darling-Hammond, L. (2022). Section introduction: Retention. In *Handbook of research on teachers of color and indigenous teachers* (p. 811). American Educational Research Association.

Cioè-Peña, M. (2018). *"Yo soy su Mama:" Latinx mothers raising emergent bilinguals labeled as dis/abled*. City University of New York.

Connor, D. (2012). Does dis/ability now sit at the table (s) of social justice and multicultural education? A descriptive survey of three recent anthologies. *Disability Studies Quarterly, 32*(3). https://dsq-sds.org/index.php/dsq/article/view/1770/3095

Cooc, N., & Yang, M. (2016). Diversity and equity in the distribution of teachers with special education credentials: Trends from California. *AERA Open, 2*(4), 1–15.

Cormier, C. J., & Scott, L. A. (2021). Castaways on Gilligan's island: Minoritized special education teachers of color advocating for equity. *Teaching Exceptional Children, 53*(3), 234–242.

Domingo, C. R., Gerber, N. C., Harris, D., Mamo, L., Pasion, S. G., Rebanal, R. D., & Rosser, S. V. (2022). More service or more advancement: Institutional barriers to academic success for women and women of color faculty at a large public comprehensive minority-serving state university. *Journal of Diversity in Higher Education, 15*(3), 365.

Echevarria, D. (2023). Nearly one-fourth of SFUSD teachers not fully credentialed, grand jury says. *San Francisco Chronicle.* https://www.sfchronicle.com/sf/article/san-francisco-teacher-shortage-grand-jury-report–18154609.php

Fenwick, L. T., & Akua, C. (2022). Section introduction: Minority-serving institutions. In *Handbook of research on teachers of color and indigenous teachers* (p. 233). American Educational Research Association.

Gist, C. D., & Bristol, T. J. (Eds.). (2022). *Handbook of research on teachers of color and indigenous teachers.* American Educational Research Association.

Gist, C. D., Bianco, M., & Lynn, M. (2019). Examining grow your own programs across the teacher development continuum: Mining research on teachers of color and nontraditional educator pipelines. *Journal of Teacher Education, 70*(1), 13–25.

González, T., Kulkarni, S., & Tefera, A. A. (2024). Centering culturally relevant and sustaining special education preparation. In *Handbook of research on special education teacher preparation* (pp. 145–166). Routledge.

Greenberg Motamedi, J., Merrill, B., Amor, H. B. H., Leong, M., & Schultz, J. L. (2019). *Educator field placement in rural areas: A policy brief for the Washington State Legislature.* Washington Student Achievement Council.

Kafka, J. (2011). *The history of "zero tolerance" in American public schooling.* Palgrave Macmillan.

Kemper, P. S., & Arturo, S. F. (2022). Exploring the relationship between demographic isolation and professional experiences of Black and Latinx teachers. *Journal of Education Human Resources, 40*(2), 138–168.

Kulkarni, S. S. (2021). Special education teachers of color and their beliefs about dis/ability and race: Counter-stories of smartness and goodness. *Curriculum Inquiry, 51*(5), 496–521. https://doi.org/10.1080/03626784.2021.1938973

Kulkarni, S. S., & Hanley-Maxwell, C. (2015). Preservice teachers' student teaching experiences in east Africa. *Teacher Education Quarterly, 42*(4), 59–81. http://www.jstor.org/stable/teaceducquar.42.4.59

Kulkarni, S. S., Bland, S., & Gaeta, J. M. (2022). From support to action: A critical affinity group of special education teachers of color. *Teacher Education and Special Education, 45*(1), 43–60.

Kulkarni, S. S., Burkhard, T., & Johns, D. J. (2024). The role of intersectionality in research on teachers of color and indigenous teachers. *Education Policy Analysis Archives, 32*, 1–16.

Kulkarni, S. S., Miller, A. L., Nusbaum, E. A., Pearson, H., & Brown, L. X. (2023). Toward disability-centered, culturally sustaining pedagogies in teacher education. *Critical Studies in Education, 65*, 107–127.

Ladson-Billings, G. (2022). *The dreamkeepers: Successful teachers of African American children*. John Wiley & Sons.

Michelman, V., Price, J., & Zimmerman, S. D. (2022). Old boys' clubs and upward mobility among the educational elite. *The Quarterly Journal of Economics*, 137(2), 845–909.

Moore, B. A. (2018). Developing special educator cultural awareness through critically reflective professional learning community collaboration. *Teacher Education and Special Education*, 41(3), 243–253. https://doi.org/10.1177/0888406418770714

Morales, A. R., Espinoza, P. S., & Duke, K. B. (2022). What exists and "what i need": In search of critical, empowering, and race-conscious approaches to mentoring from the perspective of Latina/o/x teachers. In *Handbook of research on teachers of color and indigenous teachers* (pp. 441–458). American Educational Research Association.

National Center for Education Statistics (NCES). (2019). https://nces.ed.gov/

Paris, D., & Alim, H. S. (Eds.). (2017). *Culturally sustaining pedagogies: Teaching and learning for justice in a changing world*. Teachers College Press.

Santamaría, L. J., Santamaría, C. C., & Fletcher, T. V. (2009). Journeys in cultural competency: Pre-service US teachers in Mexico study-abroad programs. *Diaspora, Indigenous, and Minority Education*, 3(1), 32–51.

Santamaría-Graff, C., Manlove, J., Stuckey, S., & Foley, M. (2020). Examining pre-service special education teachers' biases and evolving understandings about families through a family as faculty approach. *Preventing School Failure: Alternative Education for Children and Youth*, 65(1), 20–37.

Scott, L. A. (2016). Where are all the black male special education teachers? *Penn GSE Perspectives on Urban Education*, 13(1), 42–48.

Scott, L. A. (2019). Experience of Black male special education teachers: Are alternative licensure programs the desired route for recruitment and preparation? *Education and Urban Society*, 51(3), 332–350.

Scott, L. A., & Alexander, Q. (2019). Strategies for recruiting and retaining Black male special education teachers. *Remedial and Special Education*, 40(4), 236–247.

Scott, L. A., Bell, N., Dayton, M., Bowman, R. W., Evans, I., Grillo, M., Spence, C., & Layden, S. J. (2023). Special education teachers of color retention decisions: Findings from a national study. *Exceptional Children*, 89(3), 256–274.

Siuty, M. B., & Atwood, A. (2022). Intersectional disruptor: A special educator of color living and teaching in the intersections. *Teacher Education and Special Education*, 45(1), 61–76.

Siuty, M. B., Beneke, M. R., & Handy, T. (2024). Conceptualizing white-ability saviorism: A necessary reckoning with ableism in urban teacher education. *Review of Educational Research*, 95, 505–535.

Skiba, R. J., & Rausch, M. K. (2013). Zero tolerance, suspension, and expulsion: Questions of equity and effectiveness. In *Handbook of classroom management* (pp. 1073–1100). Routledge.

Skiba, R. J., Poloni-Staudinger, L., Gallini, S., Simmons, A. B., & Feggins-Azziz, R. (2006). Disparate access: The disproportionality of African American students with disabilities across educational environments. *Exceptional Children*, 72(4), 411–424.

Thornton, B., Peltier, G., & Medina, R. (2007). Reducing the special education teacher shortage. *The Clearing House: A Journal of Educational Strategies, Issues and Ideas*, 80(5), 233–238.

Trainor, A. A., Bettini, E., & Scott, L. A. (2019). Introduction to the special issue— A necessary step in pursuit of equity: Developing a racially/ethnically diverse special education teaching force. *Remedial and Special Education, 40*(4), 195–198. https://doi.org/10.1177/0741932519843176

Tyler, N. C., Yzquierdo, Z., Lopez-Reyna, N., & Flippin, S. S. (2004). Cultural and linguistic diversity and the special education workforce: A critical overview. *The Journal of Special Education, 38*, 22–38.

Villegas, A. M., Strom, K., & Lucas, T. (2012). Closing the racial/ethnic gap between students of color and their teachers: An elusive goal. *Equity & Excellence in Education, 45*(2), 283–301.

Voltz, D. L. (1998). Cultural diversity and special education teacher preparation: Critical issues confronting the field. *Teacher Education and Special Education, 21*, 63–70.

2

LAVEDA

A Black, Female Preschool Special Education Teacher Building Classroom Community

With Contributions by LaVeda Harris

> *She has been continued to be told she is not good enough, not smart enough, and that she does not deserve to let her light shine.*
> *(Perlow, et al., 2017, p. 30)*

Black and Brown bodies are being policed and surveilled in U.S. public schools (Annamma & Morrison, 2018; Ritchie, 2017). As a result of this hypersurveillance, Black and Brown children are also often excluded from classroom and school spaces, and their health and well-being are rendered invisible. Annamma and Morrison (2018) call schools "dysfunctional educational ecologies" to highlight the underrepresentation of multiply marginalized students in programs such as Advanced Placement (AP) and Gifted and Talented Education and overrepresentation in special education programs (Barrio, 2021; Voulgarides et al., 2021) and exclusionary disciplinary spaces (Cooper et al., 2022). A restructuring of school spaces to specifically center experiences of multiply marginalized students would require drawing upon the lived experiences and everyday knowledge that they provide (Paris, 2012; Paris & Alim, 2017; Ladson-Billings, 2009; Spratt & Florian, 2015); designing curriculum to engage power and justice (de los Ríos et al., 2015; Love, 2019; Romero et al., 2009); and building authentic classroom relationships among students and teachers (Duncan-Andrade, 2009).

Love (2019) emphasizes the importance of cultivating Black joy in the classroom and disrupting educational inequities through abolitionist teaching, a framework that attends to these issues of representation, relationships, and affirmation. The work needs to begin *early*, as students of color

DOI: 10.4324/9781003653783-3

endure a lifetime of racism. An undervalued and overlooked source of cultivating joy for multiply marginalized disabled children in preschools and early childhood settings is preschool special education teachers of color. They are the first teachers that multiply marginalized disabled children of color will have outside of their family and community and serve as a pivotal source of connection between children's homes and school. Black early childhood special education (ECSE) teachers, in particular, can provide a source of Black joy through representation and authenticity via shared experiences and cultural repertoires by bridging children's backgrounds and universally designing spaces of access in classrooms.

It is important to illustrate the brilliance of Black ECSE teachers to reframe existing narratives and cultivate Black joy in Black childhoods. For example, Black girls are rarely allowed to have girlhoods (Morris, 2016), and Black, female special education teachers have been socially positioned through deficit lenses in teacher education programs despite their double consciousness (Du Bois, 1903) with respect to intersectional racism and ableism. In special education teacher credential programs, Black teachers are expected to conform to learning about historical, legal, instructional, and assessment practices that render multiply marginalized disabled children invisible or, worse, deficient (Boveda & McCray, 2021). This adherence to whiteness and ableism further marginalizes their critical work and the joy they can bring to early learning. It further positions both Black ECSE teachers and multiply marginalized disabled children as socially and academically inferior.

In special education, both in P-12 schools and higher education institutions, Blackness is consistently pathologized (Boveda & McCray, 2021). Drawing from historical contexts in which Du Bois (1924) noted the comparisons of cranial sizes among Blacks and Whites to prove Black intellectual inferiority, we can see parallels in the consistent devaluing of Black and Brown knowledge and experience in teacher education (Kohli & Pizarro, 2016). For the education and preparation of teachers, opportunities, and experiences that deconstruct racist/sexist/gendered and ableist practices in schools are often reserved for teachers outside of special education (Kulkarni, 2021). Part of this pathologization and devaluing of Black knowledge comes directly from the ontological positioning in behaviorism and positivism (Gallagher, 2014). A direct consequence of these reservations is that Black special education teachers specifically, and special education teachers of color generally, are left disengaged from coursework and pedagogical strategies and practices that are critical to working as agents of resistance in schools (Kohli & Pizarro, 2022).

LaVeda is a Black female ECSE teacher and is an important part of a population of teachers who have been overlooked and underserved (Kulkarni,

2021) in both the literature and the field: special education teachers of color. Highlighting the narratives of Black teachers is crucial to interpreting schooling experiences and how school positions Black girls and girlhood (Drew et al., 2022). It is important that Black teachers are able to interpret and negotiate their own experiences to inform their pedagogical approaches toward race at the intersection of disability. In this chapter, therefore, we argue that Black, female ECSE teachers are undervalued in the broader literature of special education and teacher education, and therefore, their practices and experiences need to be centered. Additionally, while not necessarily true of all Black teachers, it is important to highlight critical Black, female ECSE teachers who are cultivating joy in the lives of their multiply marginalized disabled students. Overall, we need more narratives centering these experiences.

This chapter presents a narrative of LaVeda, a Black, female ECSE teacher who works in a large school district in Southern California, in her own words. We shift between first and third person as I, LaVeda, share my own narrative and experiences, and I, Saili, lend analysis to LaVeda's story and the ways in which she expertly navigates the systemic challenges of working to center race and disability in the curriculum with multiply marginalized disabled preschool children. LaVeda's narrative draws from her participation in a special education teacher education credential program at a Hispanic Serving Institution (HSI), her memories as a Black girl in P-12 schools, and her descriptions of her work as a preschool teacher. We use DisCrit (Annamma et al., 2013) to analyze how her work positions her through race, ability, and disability, and how she cultivates resistance and joy in her classroom by centering disability and race in her curriculum and instruction.

Background and History: Teaching Where You Live

I was born in Compton, California, at a time when my city had already experienced white flight. Before World War II, Compton was a mostly white city (Feder-Haugabook, 2017), and there were restrictions on Black people from even being able to live there. In the 1940s and 1950s, some Black families were affluent enough to move to Compton, but after that time, white flight started to happen. Many white families started to feel threatened or worried about Black people driving down property prices and left our city. In addition, the Watts Riots that took place in 1965 meant that more Black people wanted to leave central Los Angeles and move to Compton (Feder-Haugabook, 2017). The introduction of crack and cocaine, coupled with growing gang violence, shifted the image of

Compton as a mostly Black and Latino place. Though crime has gone down recently, Compton continues to struggle with lots of underemployment, and our image remains fraught with some challenges. Despite the challenges, however, I take great pride in my city, my neighborhood, and the Black community with whom I grew up and also see the heart where there is struggle.

Although I attended mostly Black public and religious schools as a child, I learned early on that school was equal to compliance. For example, I went to an all-Black preschool, which was religious and authoritarian in nature. We were expected to follow the rules and stay quiet and obedient. Back then, if and when you didn't do that, you'd get swatted. It wasn't just about following the rules, but compliance and control. Already at this young age, we were being prepped for how we were supposed to be perceived by the world. For Black people, we're told by the "good schools" that we're supposed to be quiet and obedient to get ahead and succeed in this white world. I questioned this kind of thinking as I attended schools and also as I had my own kids and thought about what I wanted for them and their futures. My experiences growing up really solidified for me that I wanted to be an educator and to work with students who needed more from school: Black and Brown children with disabilities.

I knew that I wanted to stay, to work with Black and Brown children who grew up where I grew up, and hopefully change the ways in which they see and experience school. This helped me to shape how I wanted to approach my classroom. Because my experiences in school pushed me to talk and act in ways that were associated with white people, which was attributed to success, I wanted to flip that around and make sure that the Black and Brown children with disabilities that I work with get to know themselves and celebrate their culture, race, language, and other backgrounds. Part of this for me meant that I needed to focus on representation so that my students see themselves in the school curriculum.

I come from a family of teachers. One of the biggest influences in my work is my aunt, who worked as a special education teacher. For a little while, when I was in high school, I attended her school and would get to see how her classroom was set up and how she worked with her mostly Black and Brown students with disabilities. She had this natural way about her, a genuine empathy and caring that she applied to her work, and it was just infectious. Her spirit just resonated with me, even back then in high school, and I think that's probably when I knew that I would become a teacher. I was lucky to have seen strong, Black female teachers growing up and into my first position as a paraeducator, and these role models really helped me become the kind of teacher I envisioned.

Integrating Connection and Representation

After obtaining my bachelor's degree, I stayed out of school for a while, mostly working as a paraprofessional educator in schools. When I decided to go back, I was unsure of what to expect out of being back in a university setting. I met Dr. K (Saili) at the MSI that I attended for my credential courses in ECSE. I decided to start by taking a summer course that focused on diversity and language in special education with Dr. K. I was pleasantly surprised to learn that the class spoke about race and school injustices, and I became excited about her passion for this work. We read about these urban narratives in the class[1] that focused on the lives of real Black and Brown students with disabilities: high schoolers and their real experiences. Seeing how teaching could also integrate race and disability and directly address the injustices I've thought about but never really connected in this way before fired me up to do this work!

Much of the readings in these kinds of courses from my credential and master's program provided me with the tools with which to understand and address the injustices I have experienced and seen in the classrooms where I've worked. For disability specifically, I learned from the first-person narratives of people who had been labeled in schools and experienced disability. We heard through Skype sessions from disability activists, watched videos about students with disabilities growing up, and connected with the author of Urban Narratives in Dr. K's class.

As a first step to think about disability and my students in a new way, I knew that I would set up my classroom based on dialogic listening. I wanted to listen to the students in my class, their families, and communities and hear from them about what it has been like figuring out how to address the child's disability. It's often so easy for us to assume that we know the intentions and the histories of our students and their families, when in fact there are so many layers to their stories, just as there are to my own.

Beyond listening and learning from my students, their families, and communities, I wanted students to be able to share themselves in the classroom. Using the video Star Student of the Day[2] that I was shown in a credential course as an example, I wanted my students to be able to showcase their individual preferences and build connections. With students who may have more complex disabilities and needs, the activity shown in the video needs to be modified a little bit. They may need to have larger visuals depicting the different foods, drinks, animals, and so forth. They may also need to use a voice output or sign language to share, if not vocally. We can build these supports into the activity to make it more accessible for all learners. We can also spend time learning about student preferences that may be unfamiliar to each other. For example, I have students who have immigrated from different countries and may have grown up eating foods that other students may not know about. Students might also need to explain dietary restrictions or allergies. We can build these differences into the activity so that students learn more deeply about their peers, their cultural backgrounds, and their specific needs.

Next, I wanted to showcase or highlight texts and materials that integrated and embraced the differences that my students brought with them into the classroom. For example, students in my classroom read books like *Hair Love* by Matthew A. Cherry (2019), *We Move Together* by Kelly Fritsch (2021), Anne McGuire, and Eduardo Trejos, and *Just Like Me* by Vanessa Brantley-Newton (2020) on a regular basis so that we don't just have the one diversity book but so that every one of them feels fully recognized and celebrated for who they are across race, disability, language, and so forth. *Hair Love* includes both a celebration of Black hair and a celebration of Black father-daughter relationships. Both of these areas have been heavily stereotyped about the Black community, and therefore we need to undo those kinds of harmful perspectives. *Just Like Me* uses poetry to celebrate girls of color and their emotions, their relationships with their families, and their relationships with their own bodies. *We Move Together* celebrates different kinds of backgrounds, abilities, and disabilities, and how people move and use space. I really enjoy using this book because it moves beyond disability as an inspiration to really think about how different types of people can work together cooperatively and harmoniously.

Using tools like ClassDojo,[3] I am also able to share the titles of books and materials from class with students' families so that parents and caretakers are aware of and utilize the same materials we use from class in their homes. I also ask them if they can recommend any books or materials from their language or culture that we can bring into the classroom so that we're drawing on their knowledge and cultures when we choose new books or materials.

Overall, I think that my approach to representation starts with the *dialogic listening* to the experiences that my students and their families/communities bring in when it comes to things like their cultures, backgrounds, and thoughts about disabilities. This means taking a step back and moving from being the teacher to being the learner. Next, I integrate ways for us to build classroom relationships by giving each student *opportunities to share their likes, dislikes, and preferences*. We use these to then build connections across students and to learn about any new items that student's reference in their sharing. Third, I integrate *representative literature* and stories into the preschool classroom so that students can see themselves in these books and feel celebrated for who they are. This literature might come from diverse

38 Racism and Ableism in the Classroom and Teacher Education

TABLE 2.1 Summary of Connection and Representation Practices

Practice	Description	Reframing	Example
Dialogic Listening	Describes the importance of learning from families, communities, and students about their perspectives on their learning and backgrounds.	This practice reframes existing narratives that (1) teachers hold all the knowledge of their students and (2) dialogic listening is equivalent to compliance behaviors such as tracking the speaker, sitting in attention, nodding in acknowledgment, etc. LaVeda reframes this practice to listen to the community and shift from teacher-centered expectations to learner-centered practices.	**Home Visits:** arrange a time to visit students' homes to learn more about their environment outside of school. **Pre-IEP:** arrange to meet or chat on the phone with families before an IEP meeting to learn about disability perspectives and visions for student learning.
Sharing and Using Preferences	Describes how teachers must learn about the individual preferences of their students. This means learning about their individual likes and dislikes generally and as they relate to learning.	This practice reframes the notion that teachers use indirect ways of learning about students' preferences instead of asking them directly and integrating these preferences directly into their learning.	**Star Student for a Day:** Give students an opportunity to interview their peers about their interests and use that information to guide instruction. **Learning Survey:** Provide students and families with a brief survey to share how they learn (students) and communicate (families) best and incorporate these ideas into designing instruction and communicating learning.

(Continued)

TABLE 2.1 (Continued)

Practice	Description	Reframing	Example
Representation	Integrates curriculum and literature that decenters whiteness in the classroom and celebrates all forms of difference.	This practice moves away from literature that centers white, able-bodied, middle-class, English-speaking as the normative center for curriculum and literature.	**Representative Books:** Incorporate books that celebrate differences in hair texture, skin color, body size, and ability to promote student exposure and embrace.

sets of books, such as the ones I mentioned above, or might come directly from the families themselves.

Supporting Behavior and Communication Universally

When I arrived at my current school, I immediately saw a disconnect between the policies in place and the practices that teachers and leaders were implementing with students. The school claimed to use a Multi-Tiered Systems of Support (MTSS) process, where students would move through the Response to Intervention (RTI) process, providing extra supports for those who needed intensive instruction, moderate support for those who needed some support, and whole-group support for the majority of students (Johnson et al., 2006). MTSS aims to embed ideas such as positive behavior supports or restorative justice practices as part of the systems in place at school (Hoover & deBettencourt, 2018). What I saw in practice, however, was a complete disconnect from these ideas. I saw teachers belittling and yelling at students, I saw Black and Brown students with disabilities being isolated or separated from peers for misbehavior, and I saw students being generally condescended to. This was also happening in a school that includes majority of Black and Brown students and teachers/staff. Like some of my own experiences in school here in Compton, the framework from which many of my colleagues were operating centered on compliance and obedience.

This framework of obedience and compliance differed from my own perspectives of behavior and discipline approaches. I always ask: how can children learn in fear? In the first few schools I worked with, I learned an approach that is complementary to positive behavioral intervention support called Multi-Element Behavior Support (MEBS; Doody, 2009).

40 Racism and Ableism in the Classroom and Teacher Education

This approach focuses more specifically on students with complex support needs from a humanizing stance and individualizes how behavior communicates meaning, especially for those for whom communication is nonverbal. When I adopted this approach in my classroom, other colleagues could see it displayed and learned about this way of thinking about discipline and behavior. I had visuals all around my classroom that depict the physical environment; there are cues for how to transition from activities, line up for recess, and so forth. I share this because MEBs are helpful for me to integrate in my classroom with my students, and they helped to spark conversations that allowed my colleagues to rethink some of the harsh practices they were integrating with their students.

Anytime I am thinking about behavior and discipline with my little ones, I am constantly thinking about what the impacts will be on them. If I were to isolate a student, how would it make them feel? If my words meant that a student felt hurt, stigmatized, or afraid to learn, then I am not being the kind of teacher that I committed to being. I actively consider my students, their individual needs, and their backgrounds when I design classroom-wide policies around behavior and discipline. Over the past year, I had some opportunities to participate in focus groups that reframed discipline approaches for young Black and Brown children with disabilities. In talking to parents, teachers, and administrators committed to this work, I also started to integrate practices that focused on helping students to communicate their needs in appropriate ways, self-regulate, and think of our classroom space as a safe, supportive, and caring environment for expression.

For example, I adapted a restorative wheel visual called Replacement Skills Teaching (see Figure 2.1) with my students that indicated choices for some of their commonly expressed needs, such as needing a break, wanting to stand up or sit down, wanting water, and so forth. Integrating the Replacement Skills tool into our daily routine has helped students to self-regulate their behavior with a visual cue. Students look to the Replacement Skills visual as a reminder when they feel anxious or frustrated and can then choose an outlet that matches their needs. Students can also help their peers to figure out what they might need. One of my students, who was having a bit of a meltdown in class, was shown our visual by another student in class. Pointing to the visual, they asked the student, "Do you need a break, maybe try breathing in and out?" and the student, wiping away their tears, responded with "yes" and was guided by staff to take a few deep breaths and then a designated break space in our classroom, which has some beanbag chairs and sensory toys.

Another way that my approach has shifted includes helping students see why a particularly challenging behavior might not be the best approach

FIGURE 2.1 Replacement Skills Teaching

to take during conflicts. For example, when one of my students pushed another student, they were engaged in a small conflict. First, we separated the students from each other to give them time to calm down. Then we followed up by asking students to discuss what happened. We asked the student why they chose to push their peer. They indicated it was because the peer was "in the way." We then asked them to choose another strategy for if someone gets in the way. We came up with a few sample sentences that the student could use instead of pushing, such as "I need space" or "I would like to go there" or "excuse me." The staff and I helped the student to use this approach and try it out. We also encouraged the student to apologize to their peer for the initial harm caused. We are hopeful that taking this extra time can be preventative of some of these kinds of incidents in the future.

Therefore, my discipline approach had to shift away from what I experienced as a child and some of the compliance-based approaches I saw happening in my school. MEBs gave me a good foothold on which to ground my approaches. From there, I have slowly started to move toward more restorative approaches, like *using a Replacement Skills tool with choices to help students self-regulate* their needs. This Replacement Skills tool helps my students to learn about communicating their needs in a healthy way and teaches them to do this whenever they start to feel upset, angry, frustrated, or anxious. We've also implemented communication activities to help students understand *why a particular behavior might be harmful and help students to reframe or choose a different option.* I recognize that for me this is all a work in progress and that not everything will work the same way with each child all the time. This is why the foundation I've built with families and the classroom community (students and staff) has become so important. Even if things don't always go smoothly with behavior, we can refer back to our community to repair and rebuild because we have that foundation.

Cultivating Joy in the Early Childhood Special Education Classroom

Joy is at the center of my teaching. My students dance, they move, they sing, they laugh, they create, and we have a space where all of this is welcomed. In a world where so much of my own education and the education of my students have been hyper-focused on getting them to comply and obey, I am grateful that I can build a joyful and supportive space for them in my classroom. My Black and Brown students with disabilities are too well aware of the harsh realities of life. They are often at the direct center of things like systemic racism and ableism (Kulkarni, 2021).

Although there is much to contend with in schools, I believe that my students look forward to coming to preschool and that their families are happy that we have built a strong foundation and community in our classroom. Joy takes many forms in my classroom. It can mean that students feel free to move their bodies without feeling restrictions such as the need to always be still. It can mean that students can feel safe to express themselves in the classroom; they can wear their hair and clothes in ways that are celebrated by our class community and the curriculum. It means students can have different kinds of disabilities, and that we'll always make sure that they are supported and included.

Although there were many of my own experiences growing up that were challenging in schools, I also take pride and joy in the strong Black women like my aunt who taught me how to cultivate joy in the classroom. Seeing how she navigated difficult situations that were presented by school and still focused on her students and offering them a caring space to feel welcomed, it really taught me the importance of these aspects of learning. This, coupled with some of the tools to combat injustice that I learned through some of the readings and supportive strategies in my credential program, has led me to focus my energies on creating a classroom climate that nurtures Black and Brown students with disabilities.

TABLE 2.2 Summary of Humanizing Behavior and Communication Practices

Practice	Description	Reframing	Example
Replacement Skills Tool of the MEB	In this instance, it describes how students are provided with choices for self-regulating behavior.	Reframes the narrative that behaviors must be "dealt with" by adults and allows students to self-regulate their needs through visual choices.	**Restorative Justice Wheel:** The traditional restorative justice wheel is a peacebuilding diagram that provides alternatives to physical harm or punitive reactions to behavior. For students with disabilities, this is reframed to also include self-regulatory choices such as needs for breaks or bodily needs (e.g., thirst, hunger, bathroom break).

(*Continued*)

44 Racism and Ableism in the Classroom and Teacher Education

TABLE 2.2 (Continued)

Practice	Description	Reframing	Example
Understanding what behavior communicates and why	Allows for additional time to understand why a child has engaged in a harmful behavior and how it might be replaced with a more peaceful approach.	Reframes the punitive approach to harmful behavior that focuses on exclusion, reaction, and reciprocating harm.	**Bug and a Wish:** Giving students sentence starters such as "It bugs me when. . ." and "I wish you would. . .instead" which allows students to self-advocate needs and allows those that harmed to reframe their behavior.
Cultivating joyful learning	Allows for students to be themselves in their own bodies and minds.	Reframes the narratives that children should be obedient, quiet, and still.	**Movement Opportunities:** Students are allowed to move around the classroom, and students with repetitive body movements are allowed to use these movements without consequence to enact joy and freedom.

Concluding Thoughts

Black, female ECSE teachers are an important population that have been overlooked and underserved in the literature and field of special education. Narratives of Black ECSE teachers are crucial to interpreting schooling experiences and descriptions of how Black teachers, especially Black women, are positioned in schools. It is, therefore, important to share how critical Black ECSE teachers like LaVeda interpret and negotiate their own experiences as well as the critical pedagogical approaches they use to undo racism and ableism in schools. Highlighting DisCrit Tenet Four, we privilege LaVeda's story and the intentional ways in which she works to integrate critical representation and community in her classroom and cultivates joy with her multiply marginalized disabled preschool students. We also center how LaVeda employs resistance by centering the lives, experiences, and stories of her students, their families, and their communities (DisCrit Tenet Seven).

First, LaVeda cultivates teacher agency by deviating not only from her own educational history, which was marked with themes of compliance and rigidity, but also from her own practices at a school site that often promotes zero-tolerance discipline policies and deficit views of multiply marginalized disabled students of color. LaVeda's work to undo these harmful practices demonstrates a resilience and dedication to the lives of multiply marginalized disabled students of color.

Second, LaVeda holds high expectations for all of her students, as is a hallmark of culturally relevant pedagogy (Ladson-Billings, 1995). Her belief in her students' abilities to learn and flourish and to seek out extensive resources to support her students is a key aspect of high-quality teachers of color (Blazar, 2021; Ladson-Billings, 2022). It is critical that narratives of special education teachers of color, like broader narratives of teachers of color (Gist & Bristol, 2022), illustrate their effectiveness in order to expand the educational workforce and to draw from the critical practices of these teachers.

Third, LaVeda's story highlights the tensions and challenges of teachers of color who work in oppressive systems of schooling such as public school special education spaces, where students may have one teacher, such as LaVeda who can challenge these systems independently with her students but risks losing them to zero tolerance policies when they move on to other classrooms and schools. In a system that has a deeply embedded sense of privileging whiteness and controlling Black and Brown bodies, it is worth examining whether Black, ECSE teachers such as LaVeda can be sustained through such a system.

Lastly, LaVeda's story also highlights the importance of multiply marginalized disabled youth of color and their experiences of joy within a harsh and heavily oppressive system. A mark of a teacher who is truly engaged in abolitionist teaching and resistance to this oppression, LaVeda cultivates joy with her students through opportunities for dialogic listening, movement, affirmation, access, and self-determination. Further exploration is needed to see how the students themselves experience these practices and how they may develop stronger identities or self-concepts as a result of LaVeda's dedication. What is clear, however, is that LaVeda's exemplar is a way to emphasize the importance of special education teachers of color and their critical work in schools.

Notes

1 Connor, D. J. (2008). *Urban narratives: Portraits in progress, life at the intersections of learning disability, race, & social class* (Vol. 5). Peter Lang.
2 "Star student of the day." *The teaching channel*. https://learn.teachingchannel. com/video/building-classroom-community?gclid=CjwKCAjwsfuYBhAZEiwA5a

46 Racism and Ableism in the Classroom and Teacher Education

6CDF_HgJ2Dsyv6y406z9CLHtV3dLv5FKt5FJDNBakruVmy8qfNABOXiRoC-S7sQAvD_BwE
3 https://classdojo.com/

References

Annamma, S., & Morrison, D. (2018). DisCrit classroom ecology: Using praxis to dismantle dysfunctional education ecologies. *Teaching and Teacher Education, 73*, 70–80. https://doi.org/10.1016/j.tate.2018.03.008

Annamma, S. A., Connor, D., & Ferri, B. (2013). Dis/ability critical race studies (DisCrit): Theorizing at the intersections of race and dis/ability. *Race Ethnicity and Education, 16*(1), 1–31. https://doi.org/10.1080/13613324.2012.730511

Barrio, B. L. (2021). Understanding culturally responsive practices in teacher preparation: An avenue to address disproportionality in special education. *Teaching Education, 32*(4), 437–456. https://doi.org/10.1080/10476210.2020.1796956

Blazar, D. (2021). *Teachers of color, culturally responsive teaching, and student outcomes: Experimental evidence from the random assignment of teachers to classes* [EdWorkingPaper: 21–501]. Annenberg Institute at Brown University. https://doi.org/10.26300/jym0-wz02

Boveda, M., & McCray, E. D. (2021). Writing (for) our lives: Black feminisms, interconnected guidance, and qualitative research in special education. *International Journal of Qualitative Studies in Education*, 1–19. https://doi.org/10.1080/09518398.2020.1771465

Brantley-Newton, V. (2020). *Just like me*. Knopf Books for Young Readers.

Cherry, M. A. (2019). *Hair love*. Kokila.

Connor, D. J. (2008). *Urban narratives: Portraits in progress, life at the intersections of learning disability, race, & social class* (Vol. 5). Peter Lang.

Cooper, S. M., Burnett, M., Golden, A., Butler-Barnes, S., & Inniss-Thompson, M. (2022). School discrimination, discipline inequities, and adjustment among Black adolescent girls and boys: An intersectionality-informed approach. *Journal of Research on Adolescence, 32*(1), 170–190. https://doi.org/10.1111/jora.12716

de los Ríos, C. V., Lopez, J., & Morrell, E. (2015). Toward a critical pedagogy of race: Ethnic studies and literacies of power in high school classrooms. *Race and Social Problems, 7*(1), 84–96. https://doi.org/10.1007/s12552-014-9142-1

Doody, C. (2009). Multi-element behaviour support as a model for the delivery of a human rights-based approach for working with people with intellectual disabilities and behaviours that challenge. *British Journal of Learning Disabilities, 37*(4), 293–299. https://doi.org/10.1111/j.1468-3156.2009.00585.x

Drew, V., Wilson, M. L., & McCarter, S. A. (2022). The overcriminalisation of Black girls: Using an intersectional lens to examine the school-to-prison pipeline. *Critical and Radical Social Work, 10*(2), 242–259. https://doi.org/10.1332/204986021X16535461234260

Du Bois, W. E. B. (1903). *The talented tenth* (pp. 102–104). James Pott and Company.

Du Bois, W. E. B. (1924). *The gift of Black folk: The Negroes in the making of America*. Stratford Company.

Duncan-Andrade, J. (2009). Note to educators: Hope required when growing roses in concrete. *Harvard Educational Review, 79*(2), 181–194. https://doi.org/10.17763/haer.79.2.nu3436017730384w

Feder-Haugabook, A. (2017). Compton, California 1867. *Blackpast.org*. https://www.blackpast.org/african-american-history/compton-california-1867/

Fritsch, K., McGuire, A., & Trejos, E. (2021). *We move together*. AK Press.

Gallagher, D. J. (2014). Challenging orthodoxy in special education: On longstanding debates and philosophical divides revisited. In *The Sage handbook of special education* (Vol. 2, pp. 819–840). SAGE Publications Ltd.

Gist, C. D., & Bristol, T. J. (Eds.). (2022). *Handbook of research on teachers of color and indigenous teachers*. American Educational Research Association.

Hoover, J. J., & DeBettencourt, L. U. (2018). Educating culturally and linguistically diverse exceptional learners: The need for continued advocacy. *Exceptionality*, *26*(3), 176–189. https://doi.org/10.1080/09362835.2017.1299530

Johnson, E., Mellard, D. F., Fuchs, D., & McKnight, M. A. (2006). *Responsiveness to intervention (RTI): How to do it* [RTI Manual]. National Research Center on Learning Disabilities.

Kohli, R., & Pizarro, M. (2016). Fighting to educate our own: Teachers of color, relational accountability, and the struggle for racial justice. *Equity & Excellence in Education*, *49*(1), 72–84. https://doi.org/10.1080/10665684.2015.1121457

Kohli, R., & Pizarro, M. (2022). The layered toll of racism in teacher education on teacher educators of color. *AERA Open*, *8*, 23328584221078538.

Kulkarni, S. S. (2021). Special education teachers of color and their beliefs about dis/ability and race: Counter-stories of smartness and goodness. *Curriculum Inquiry*, *51*(5), 496–521. https://doi.org/10.1080/03626784.2021.1938973

Ladson-Billings, G. (1995). But that's just good teaching! The case for culturally relevant pedagogy. *Theory into Practice*, *34*(3), 159–165.

Ladson-Billings, G. (2009). 'Who you callin'nappy-headed?' A critical race theory look at the construction of Black women. *Race Ethnicity and Education*, *12*(1), 87–99. https://doi.org/10.1080/13613320802651012

Ladson-Billings, G. (2022). *The dreamkeepers: Successful teachers of African American children*. John Wiley & Sons.

Love, B. L. (2019). *We want to do more than survive: Abolitionist teaching and the pursuit of educational freedom*. Beacon Press.

Morris, M. (2016). *Pushout: The criminalization of Black girls in schools*. The New Press.

Paris, D. (2012). Culturally sustaining pedagogy: A needed change in stance, terminology, and practice. *Educational Researcher*, *41*(3), 93–97. https://doi.org/10.3102/0013189X12441244

Paris, D., & Alim, H. S. (Eds.). (2017). *Culturally sustaining pedagogies: Teaching and learning for justice in a changing world*. Teachers College Press.

Perlow, O. N., Wheeler, D. I., Bethea, S. L., & Scott, B. M. (Eds.). (2017). *Black women's liberatory pedagogies: Resistance, transformation, and healing within and beyond the academy*. Springer.

Ritchie, A. J. (2017). *Invisible no more: Police violence against Black women and women of color*. Beacon press.

Romero, A., Arce, S., & Cammarota, J. (2009). A barrio pedagogy: Identity, intellectualism, activism, and academic achievement through the evolution of critically compassionate intellectualism. *Race Ethnicity and Education*, *12*(2), 217–233. https://doi.org/10.1080/13613320902995483

Spratt, J., & Florian, L. (2015). Inclusive pedagogy: From learning to action. Supporting each individual in the context of 'everybody'. *Teaching and Teacher Education*, *49*, 89–96. https://doi.org/10.1016/j.tate.2015.03.006

Voulgarides, C., Aylward, A., Tefera, A., Artiles, A. J., Alvarado, S. L., & Noguera, P. (2021). Unpacking the logic of compliance in special education: Contextual influences on discipline racial disparities in suburban schools. *Sociology of Education*, *94*(3), 208–226. https://doi.org/10.1177/00380407211013322

3

LORIANN

Integrating Disability and Race via a Restorative Lens in Elementary School

With Contributions by Loriann Casillas

> *No hay mal que por bien no venga.*
> (Elvia's abuelita in Presumed Incompetent, p. 372)

> [You can find something good coming out of something bad-eventually]

My name is Loriann Casillas, and I would like to think that I've always wanted to be a teacher or that I was inspired by one of my teachers, but the truth is a bit more complicated. Let me start by saying that my parents instilled in me a love of learning. My mama and papa read books to me every night and encouraged me to memorize those stories, aphorisms, and quotes. To this day, I can attribute my love of reading and language arts to their dedication in supporting my learning.

Unfortunately, school was not as warm and inviting as those stories in which I immersed myself. When I started school, I often felt too shy or nervous to talk in class. This led to me being dismissed or rendered invisible by my teachers. Teachers at school often either forgot that I was there or assumed that my lack of a response meant that I did not know how to speak English. Although I come from a background with family members who speak Spanish, my family and I communicated regularly in English. In some cases, this assumption that I didn't speak English well led to teachers also not believing in my ability to do the work for my classes. I was thought of as incapable of challenging curriculum and activities. Once I did find my voice, I was told I was argumentative or told to stop talking. School was a place where I couldn't win and a world I didn't want to be a part of.

DOI: 10.4324/9781003653783-4

How I Became a Special Education Teacher

The experiences I had in school as a young Latina who was dismissed, or thought of as incapable, made me feel determined that I would never step foot into another school building after graduating high school. I loved learning, but the transition from high school to college was very difficult. While attending college, I found myself pushed toward teaching. I attended community college and earned a Drug and Alcohol certificate. I was determined to earn my bachelor's degree, and I transferred to San José State University. When I became a philosophy major, I began to think about teaching and started a teacher preparation program. First, I applied to become a substitute teacher in some of the local school districts in my area. I thought this might be a way for me to continue my education while also working. In California, due to the significant teacher shortage, getting a substitute license was (and still is) pretty quick and easy; you just needed a bachelor's degree (Bruno, 2002).

I decided to take an elementary school special education substitute position that was supposed to be a temporary assignment. Little did I know how much that position would change the course of my career plan. As I began teaching, I started to feel tremendous joy and excitement derived mostly from my students and the school site. After a few short months of substitute teaching, my position as a resource specialist in special education transitioned from a temporary to a full-time teaching position. My school principal recommended that I consider getting my teaching credential in special education so that I could maintain my role full-time.

Suddenly, after years of reluctance, I was thrown into the world of special education, or as I like to call it, the world of acronyms! I began researching the Individualized Education Plan (IEP), the Individualized Family Support Plan (IFSP), and what it meant to work in either an Special Day Class (SDC) or Resource Program (RSP) in order to understand how the field of special education worked. I'm fortunate that as soon as I joined special education and started teaching my students, it started to feel incredibly natural to me. It seemed as though all of my prior jobs and experiences had led me to this point.

Challenges of Special Education Teaching

Although I felt rewarded by special education and the work I was doing, I would be remiss not to talk about some of the clear challenges faced by teachers in this field. One of the biggest challenges I noticed as I entered the field was the amount of paperwork I was expected to be responsible for and how this was also tied to compliance. For example, the position I walked into my first year involved nearly half a caseload of students who had overdue annual and triennial IEPs. Inheriting this extra work was frustrating as a new teacher still trying to learn on the job. Districts with additional resources also tend to have someone on staff to help schedule these meetings for the multiple educational stakeholders, such as parents, speech and language therapists, or school psychologists, who are required to attend. In our school district, we were doing this job of figuring out how to bring overdue IEPs into compliance while also trying to schedule upward of ten different people to attend these meetings.

An additional frustration that I noticed in special education had to do with how students with disabilities were viewed by educational professionals. Walking into my first faculty lounge as a new teacher, I was surprised to hear how some of the faculty and staff would talk about their students. The deficit views that these teachers had about their students, particularly when it came to students of color with disabilities, were disheartening. Sadly, I also saw similar patterns in the classrooms I worked with; where I would witness certain teachers call out the students of color with disabilities and make quick referrals to the office. These incidents only furthered my resolve to be a caring and restorative educator to my students. It also led to my later interest in restorative justice practices that I began to utilize with my students.

I believe that one of the biggest challenges of being in the field of special education came from being a special education teacher of color. It's important to share that despite feeling that I had found my calling, there was the isolation of being "the only at the schools where I worked." I was the only Latina teacher at my school site and the only one working in special education, even in a district as diverse as Oakland Unified. This, coupled with the general isolation of being one of only a few special education teachers at my school site, also raised challenges for building connections and collaboration.

As a whole, it is important for me to share the tensions that existed between my love for my students and the approaches I incorporated into my teaching with the broader challenges I faced as a special education teacher of color in a field that is often overwhelmingly white. I also note how some of the general challenges of special education, such as the paperwork, isolation, and deficit perceptions of students of color with disabilities, led to some difficulties as I tried to integrate more restorative justice practices with my students. It is important for me to describe how I responded to some of these challenges to continue to persist in education.

Responding to Challenges

To face these challenges, it was important for me to check in with myself, find emotional grounding, and analyze where some of my negative feelings about some of these challenges stemmed from, such as my own experiences with school. Like the families of some of my students, who may not have wanted to appear at an IEP meeting due to their own trauma with school, the trauma of my own negative experiences at school made it so I didn't really want to set foot on a school campus ever again. I took those experiences and tried to channel my energy into undoing what had been done to me in school. I have a strong belief that every child deserves a free and appropriate education and the opportunity to learn in meaningful ways in schools. These values that I uphold informed my practices as a special education teacher of color, the ways I approach teaching, and how I engage with parents and students. Every child deserves to be around adults who love and care for them and have a strong investment in their successful future. Even if other educators that I came across were not always doing this, I wanted to be sure that I maintained that stance. Thus, while there are still challenges in the field of education and the treatment of students with disabilities, entering the field felt really positive to me, as though I was ensuring that what happened to me didn't have to be the reality of other students of color and the students with disabilities that I supported. Thus, it feels like something "bien/good" did come from those early negative experiences with school.

This chapter will explore how the impact of my early experiences with schooling motivated me to engage with my students and school community in developing a restorative justice approach. Saili and I go back and forth describing my experiences as a Latina special education teacher and the only resource special education teacher at my school site. We also draw from the research on special education and some of the equity issues related to discipline for this population of students of color with disabilities. We share how restorative justice practices can be useful for all students, including students of color with disabilities, and some of the ways that I have been able to incorporate these practices in my former role as a special education teacher of color and in my current position as the vice principal of a high school.

Meeting Loriann (Saili's Perspective)

I (Saili) met Loriann about five years ago, and I recall one of our first conversations was about how she never wanted to be a teacher. School was a place where Loriann held deeply negative experiences and where she was constantly underestimated or presumed incompetent. Loriann shared with me that she barely spoke in class and that this quietness was often mistaken for a lack of comprehension. As a Latina female, teachers often assumed she had a language barrier even though English was her first language.

Loriann recalled that in high school specifically, she was accused by a teacher of cheating because her book report looked "too good." Loriann had an interest in her school's speech and debate team but was told by a high school guidance counselor that it was "too academic" for her. When she insisted that she wanted to participate, the counselor went on to say that if she failed the class, it wouldn't be removed from her transcript and she would have to "live with the F." Despite all of these negative experiences, Loriann thrived in debate, winning national awards in college. She transferred from a community college to a local four-year university, where she found professors who cared about her success and where school finally started to become a welcoming place for her.

Loriann started university as a philosophy major and got her certification for drug and addiction counseling. She worked closely with a local women's shelter and saw the direct impacts of homelessness on young children. This instilled in her a desire to continue to support children, and she decided to work as a substitute teacher in local schools. Substitute teaching while earning a teaching credential, Loriann was placed in a program supporting students with disabilities during intervention periods. She also applied to a program called CalStateTeach, which supports individuals with teaching credentials in California to move from a preliminary credential (valid for five years) to a clear credential (valid for life) (see https://www.calstateteach.net/home).

During this early point of teaching students with disabilities, the majority of whom were students of color; Loriann quickly adopted asset-based pedagogical approaches. Loriann is, in many ways, an exemplar of a special education teacher of color dedicated to her students of color with disabilities, advocating for their needs and working to undo the often deficit perspectives attached to this population of students. In the next section, Loriann and I (Saili) will share some of the critical practices that Loriann has utilized with students of color with disabilities. Her focus on restorative justice, in particular, has helped her to generate humanizing environments with her students. We begin by sharing why restorative justice practices benefit all students, but especially students of color with disabilities, who have been subject to the most segregation and harsh punishments in schools (Kulkarni & Chong, 2021). We then share how Loriann *honor's student voice* and *integrates a restorative justice lens* both in her time as a special education teacher of color and in her current role as a vice principal.

Restorative Justice Practices for Students of Color With Disabilities

Restorative justice practices have been shown to begin to undo some of the harm created by excessively harsh and punitive practices, especially those that target multiply marginalized youth (González et al., 2021). Restorative Justice (RJ) is an approach that focuses on repairing harm while holding the responsible parties accountable for their actions. The focus of RJ on repairing harm has important implications for education and reimagining how discipline approaches can look in schools, especially for students who are multiply marginalized disabled youth (Kulkarni & Chong, 2021). Pavelka (2013) described the key features of restorative justice as (1) repairing harm, which both holds the perpetrator responsible and heals those who were harmed; (2) reducing risk which gives everyone in the classroom or school community a sense of peace and safety; and (3) empowering community which makes it a collective responsibility of students, families, and educators to carry out RJ practices.

Disabled youth of color are often the targets of excessively harsh or punitive disciplinary practices in schools and have a much higher risk of becoming part of the school-to-prison nexus (Meiners, 2011; Skiba et al., 2014). This disparity can happen as early as early childhood education. Beneke and Cheatham (2020) explained how the practices, histories, and experiences that families and communities of young children of color bring into the classroom are consistently erased in favor of white norms. Often, there is an assumption that young children do not have the capacity to understand issues of race and power (Souto-Manning et al., 2022). This idea is further perpetuated for young children of color with disabilities, who are thought to not have the intellectual capacities to understand racial injustice. Souto-Manning et al. (2022) note, however, that young children absolutely internalize race and power dynamics. Additionally, disabled children of color are often directly impacted by issues of racial injustice, ableism, and power dynamics and therefore deserve to learn about how these intersecting oppressions work in schools (see Kulkarni et al., 2023).

Especially for children with more extensive support needs, there has been a consistent dehumanization, as they are often de-raced, de-gendered, and de-sexualized (Kulkarni et al., 2023). Classrooms for children with extensive, complex support needs are also spaces where the curriculum is watered down or virtually nonexistent, choice is limited, and culturally sustaining practices are ignored in favor of "race neutral" directed instruction (Kulkarni et al., 2023). In California, for example, students with extensive support needs are still overwhelmingly educated in Special Day Classes (SDCs), which are separate settings for students who identify under this classification. Even today, many are often only "mainstreamed" into a single course, and language about performance and readiness dictates how often students are permitted to participate in educational content and activities with their same-aged peers.

Special education teachers of color such as Loriann combatted these lowered expectations and dehumanizing practices for students with disabilities in California schools. As a special education teacher, Loriann moved away from traditional behavioral management and discipline techniques with her students, instead focusing on building a restorative justice classroom community. Her specific attention to generating a restorative community of learners has implications for students with extensive support needs, inclusive practices and culturally sustaining pedagogies.

For students with extensive support needs, restorative justice has the potential to undo traditional conceptions of desired behaviors in favor of expression and community. In our recent work (Kulkarni et al., 2023), we highlighted how early childhood and elementary school teachers working with students with disabilities were able to integrate restorative practices with young children with a variety of disabilities. Those who had students with extensive support needs successfully integrated adaptive versions of restorative justice practices such as giving students plenty of choice, using language and augmentative devices to reduce conflict, and generating collective versus individual behavioral responses. Therefore, special education teachers of color, such as Loriann, can use their lens of asset-based pedagogical practices to support all students with disabilities.

Loriann's view of disability as an identity expression of her students also encourages her to advocate for their continued inclusion in general education classrooms. Although SDC classrooms are still fairly common around the state of California, Loriann worked closely with her school communities to create opportunities for inclusion. Her interest in supporting inclusion goes hand-in-hand with her dedication toward culturally sustaining pedagogies. Built around a framework of restorative justice, Loriann believes that all students of color with disabilities can learn alongside their peers with curriculum that is meaningfully centering their livelihoods.

In our 2022 paper, we (Kulkarni & Chong, 2021) found that teachers such as Loriann, who work as teachers of color supporting multiply marginalized young children with disabilities, have incorporated RJ practices in meaningful ways with their students and utilize RJ practices as a lens for navigating classroom and school spaces generally. Additionally, Loriann's work as a special education teacher of color sought to decenter whiteness and ableism in the elementary classroom. She believed that students, even the elementary-aged children with whom she worked (multiply marginalized disabled youth), deserve to learn about race, power, and ableism and how it operates in schools. Below we share some examples of how Loriann incorporated RJ practices with both her students with disabilities and broadly as she worked as a special education teacher of color at her school site.

Having had no prior special education teaching experiences, Loriann spent her first year as a teacher acclimating to a new language, population of students, and school setting. Incredibly, however, one thing that her first school site had was an integrated approach to restorative justice. At her first school site, Loriann noticed how participation in restorative justice circles was not just reserved for students who had challenging behavior, but for everyone, including the teachers and staff. Seeing how school could be a welcoming and supportive environment for the entire community, unlike her own experiences of school being a harmful place, changed Loriann's perspectives on teaching. She additionally realized that she wanted to actively be a part of making school a positive place for all students.

As a special education teacher, Loriann's early experiences working with students with a variety of educational needs continue to inform her approach to students and their behavior. Though she is currently working as a vice principal of a high school now, she carries the same practices that she developed at her first teaching site with her multiply marginalized disabled students into her new role. In the classroom, Loriann's approach to engaging in restorative practices included *honoring student voice* and *incorporating a restorative justice lens* (see Kulkarni & Chong, 2021). Mansfield (2014) notes how critical it is for educational leaders who hope to become strong student advocates to solicit student input and feedback on the policies and practices implemented in schools. Irizarry (2009) also shares how educators and leaders should move away from deficit views of needing to fix students toward including their voices in problem-solving endeavors. In this way, Loriann also worked to resist the oppressive structures of racism and ableism and cultivated a joyful classroom experience for her students where their voices were honored.

Honoring Student Voice

A hallmark of (my) Loriann's practices as a special education teacher of color is to ensure that students feel accepted for who they are in the classroom. While some teachers have written off student behavior as internal character flaws, I (Loriann) understand that all behavior is communicating a message. I have learned to connect with students in order to understand how they communicate their emotions. Additionally, I believe that my students deserve equitable access to meaningful curriculum that represents their thoughts and feelings. One of the ways that I have done this is by *honoring student voice*. Giving my students the tools with which to communicate their needs has always been a hallmark of my practice. I've also allowed them to share their perspectives on our lessons and curriculum. I am committed to the practice that learning is a joint exercise, and giving my students the space to express their views has always been a part of this. In our classroom, students bring their voice and perspective to all areas of

56 Racism and Ableism in the Classroom and Teacher Education

TABLE 3.1 Summary of Connection and Restorative Practices

Practice	Description	Reframing	Example
Honoring Student Voice	Giving students the freedom to make decisions about their behavior and learning.	Reframes the existing narrative that learning and behavior move from teacher-directed to student-directed.	Students co-create classroom rules, decorating, daily schedules, activities, and "drinking tea" dialogues, as shown in Figure 3.1.
Enacting a restorative lens	Using and modeling restorative justice practices in all parts of school, not just as it relates to the classroom and student behavior.	Reframes the existing narrative that restorative justice is a singular practice that can be implemented only in a specific context.	Conversation techniques modeling empathy and listening, curriculum reflecting values of RJ practices, RJ circles for celebrations such as birthdays or landmark events for students.
Resisting racism and ableism in schools	Students viewed via deficits and stereotypes, often excluded from activities.	Moving to an asset-based lens, supporting each individual toward inclusion and belonging.	Students led IEPs focused on assets, Student opportunities to provide feedback to teacher with RSP as support, Data conversations rooted in equity with families, community members, and teaching staff.

their learning experience, such as helping to design the classroom decor, deciding which of four tasks we start with, deciding which materials we use, and where each material has a "home" in our classroom. We also will change the layout of the classroom depending on the needs of our students. For instance, some students want to sit on the ground and use lap desks during their intervention time, while others want to sit on a wiggle chair,

FIGURE 3.1 Tea Set for "Drinking Tea" Dialogues

and some want to sit at the round table and take stretch breaks midway through the lesson. We adapt to the needs of each student while respecting each other's identities. In Figure 3.1, I also share a picture of the teapot we've used when we "drink tea" together. This activity creates a shared space where students and I can have an open dialogue about what's going on in the classroom and allows this to happen in a relaxed and familial kind of setting. I believe that by giving each of my students this autonomy, I am honoring their voices and allowing them to make decisions about their learning.

Restorative Justice Lens

I maintain the use of a *restorative justice as a lens* with which to guide my classroom and schoolwide educational practices. This means that I am

58 Racism and Ableism in the Classroom and Teacher Education

consistently incorporating restorative justice practices in all aspects of my work. For example, I use restorative justice practices in my interactions with students in my classroom, at the school, and with adults. I've learned that conflicts can be resolved using a restorative justice process across an entire school community. This means that when I've had conflicts with paraprofessionals or other teachers, we could use the same approaches that had been presented as an option to students to resolve our own issues. As shared above, I also try to create a welcoming environment for my students. Students were given autonomy and equitable sharing voice into what was important for their classroom. My students and I sometimes sit together drinking tea and deciding on what would be best for our class-room. I also do not believe in keeping a desk at the front of the classroom but rather sitting on the rug or near my students. This way we can solve problems together, collectively as a class, rather than in an authoritative manner. I believe in helping to guide my students toward creating their own solutions while providing them with the necessary tools and supports.

I believe that restorative justice is a lens that can be taken into any class-room or context. As a vice principal, I use it with my staff to resolve con-flicts and with the student body at my school site. I also used it regularly with my multiply marginalized students with disabilities when I worked as a resource specialist teacher. Restorative justice is more than just sitting around in a circle together; if we wish to live by the teachings of restora-tive justice, we need to think of it as a lens that informs everything we do. I found that this has really helped me cope with some of the more difficult conversations I've had to have with colleagues, staff, and students at my school. I am grateful to have had the experience of working with a school that really valued RJ in this way.

Resistance to Ableism and Racism

DisCrit (Annamma et al., 2013) highlights the interdependence of racism and ableism in schools. We see this in the ways students of color with disabilities are segregated from their peers, mislabeled with judgmental disability categories such as emotional behavioral disturbance, and more frequently subject to harsh or exclusionary measures of discipline. As a featured teacher in this book on special education teachers of color, Lori-ann demonstrates a different way of approaching learning and behavior for students of color with disabilities. Loriann's approach to supporting stu-dents of color with disabilities through a restorative lens included meeting students where they are, cultivating strong relationships between herself, her students, and their families, and navigating conflict.

In juxtaposition to special education teachers of color, Beneke et al. (2022) share how white teacher candidates often have the luxury of ambivalence or avoidance toward systemic racial inequities, even if these inequities are occurring around them. For many white teacher candidates and teachers, school represented a place of safety, support, and care. In the case of special education teachers of color like Loriann, however, school held the structural violence of being a space where she and her abilities were constantly underestimated.

In an effort to undo this violence, Loriann worked to integrate a restorative justice lens into her instructional approaches as a special education teacher of color. Moving away from authoritative approaches where she as the teacher was seen as knowledgeable and her multiply marginalized disabled students as deficient, Loriann integrated opportunities for student voice and generated a deeply democratic structure in her classroom where students discuss their learning outcomes and the physical environment of the classroom space collectively. In her restorative lens, students work with the teacher and peers to solve critical issues, and students are kept in the classroom rather than being sent out for behavioral challenges. Overall, as a special education teacher of color, Loriann worked to break the cycle of violence perpetuated by schools toward multiply marginalized disabled youth of color.

The Need for Community Efforts

One area of advice that I (Loriann) wish to share with new special education teachers of color is to work closely with other educators of color at your school site or to become a part of a racial affinity group. Having these kinds of supports would have absolutely made me feel less isolated in my first few years as a special education teacher and as a teacher of color. In Kulkarni et al.'s (2022) work on a critical affinity group for special education teachers of color, they noted how these spaces provided a collective healing space that these teachers would not otherwise have experienced. In my early years as an elementary special education resource teacher, I was sometimes "the only" one in a couple of different ways. I was often the only special education teacher at the site, one of only a few teachers of Latina descent, and one of the few teachers of color generally. While this in itself didn't deter me from continuing to support my students as a former special education teacher of color and current vice principal, I share this because I believe in the importance of community. Becoming a part of a community of teachers of color gave me the support I needed to turn into a teacher that I could be proud of: someone who advocates for and listens to my students,

60 Racism and Ableism in the Classroom and Teacher Education

someone who sees the best in each student, even ones who present challenging behaviors, and someone who can practice restorative justice in all aspects of my work. It also allowed me to engage in self and community care and take more joy in my role as a special education teacher of color. Specifically, I felt like I had a second family that I could look out for and who would look out for me. This, coupled with my own de-stressors such as spending time with my family, really helped to sustain me.

Conclusion

Although my experiences as a student growing up were often traumatic and structurally violent, I am grateful to be in the position to change how my students experience school. Though I was initially drawn away from ever becoming a teacher, my eventual path toward education gave me the opportunity to lean into the deep values I hold about students of color and students with disabilities. By honoring my students' voices and utilizing a restorative justice lens toward my work, I harnessed some of the power that was taken away from me as a student and sometimes as a special education teacher.

Over time, I also learned that I cannot do this critical work alone and am grateful to have built a community alongside other teachers of color who are committed to resisting oppressive practices for students of color with disabilities. Moving away from being "the only" also allowed me to experience the support I always needed in this collective fight. It's something I now carry with me into my leadership role as a vice principal, utilizing my power to support teachers of color and to continue to advocate for students of color with disabilities. I hope that this book chapter can provide similar support for those special education teachers of color who feel like they are doing this work alone.

References

Annamma, S. A., Connor, D., & Ferri, B. (2013). Dis/ability critical race studies (DisCrit): Theorizing at the intersections of race and dis/ability. *Race Ethnicity and Education*, 16(1), 1–31.

Beneke, M. R., & Cheatham, G. A. (2020). Teacher candidates talking (but not talking) about dis/ability and race in preschool. *Journal of Literacy Research*, 52(3), 245–268.

Beneke, M. R., Siuty, M. B., & Handy, T. (2022). Emotional geographies of exclusion: Whiteness and ability in teacher education research. *Teachers College Record*, 124(7), 105–130.

Bruno, J. E. (2002). The geographical distribution of teacher absenteeism in large urban school district settings: Implications for school reform efforts aimed at promoting equity and excellence in education. *Education Policy Analysis Archives*, 10(32). http://epaa.asu.edu/epaa/v10n32/

CalStateTeach. https://www.calstateteach.net/home

González, T., Epstein, R., Krelitz, C., & Shinde, R. (2021). Restorative justice, school reopenings, and educational equity: A contemporary mapping and analysis of state law. *UC Davis Law Review Online, 55*, 43.

Irizarry, J. G. (2009). Reinvigorating multicultural education through youth participatory action research. *Multicultural Perspectives, 11*, 194–199.

Kulkarni, S. S., Bland, S., & Gaeta, J. M. (2022). From support to action: A critical affinity group of special education teachers of color. *Teacher Education and Special Education, 45*(1), 43–60.

Kulkarni, S. S., & Chong, M. M. (2021). Teachers of color implementing restorative justice practices in elementary classrooms: A DisCrit analysis. *Equity & Excellence in Education, 54*(4), 378–392.

Kulkarni, S. S., Miller, A. L., Nusbaum, E. A., Pearson, H., & Brown, L. X. (2023). Toward disability-centered, culturally sustaining pedagogies in teacher education. *Critical Studies in Education, 2*, 1–21.

Mansfield, K. C. (2014). How listening to student voices informs and strengthens social justice research and practice. *Educational Administration Quarterly, 50*(3), 392–430.

Meiners, E. R. (2011). Ending the school-to-prison pipeline/building abolition futures. *The Urban Review, 43*(4), 547–565.

Pavelka, S. (2013). Practices and policies for implementing restorative justice within schools. *The Prevention Researcher, 20*(1), 15–18.

Skiba, R. J., Arredondo, M. I., & Williams, N. T. (2014). More than a metaphor: The contribution of exclusionary discipline to a school-to-prison pipeline. *Equity & Excellence in Education, 47*(4), 546–564.

Souto-Manning, M., Emerson, A. C., Marcel, G., Rabadi-Raol, A., & Turner, A. (2022). Democratizing creative early educational experiences: A matter of racial justice. *Review of Research in Education, 46*(1), 1–31.

4

SAMUEL

Navigating Identity Alongside Disabled Students of Color in Middle School

With Contributions by Samuel Bland

Erik Erikson's theory of psychosocial development (1968) suggests that identity development relies on the ability to establish a meaningful self-concept in relation to one's life experiences. Self-concept can be established through past and present experiences and inform future experiences. Identity is also impacted by one's gender, race, culture, language, socioeconomic status, sexuality, and visible/invisible disabilities (Forber-Pratt et al., 2017). Navigating identity, therefore, becomes an essential part of understanding and enacting one's beliefs and perspectives.

Teacher identity has been recognized as a critical component of the ways in which teachers make meaning of their experiences in classrooms with students and how they develop their roles in schools (Gallchóir et al., 2018). Roberts (2013), for example, found that special education teachers negotiated teaching identities through a combination of pre-service and in-service knowledge and their feelings of self-efficacy when working to provide literacy instruction to students with significant disabilities. In our recent paper (Kulkarni et al., 2022), we noted how special education teachers of color draw from a combination of their experiences as P-12 students across race and ability, their experiences as teacher candidates in a preparation program, and their present experiences in the classroom to inform their teaching identities.

In this chapter, we (Saili and Samuel) chronicle Samuel's identity as a Black, male special education teacher with a learning disability. Samuel and I share how his identity as disabled and as a Black male special education teacher informs his P-12 teaching choices working with predominantly Black and Brown disabled students in middle school. We also talk

DOI: 10.4324/9781003653783-5

about how his experiences with his own schooling, teacher credential program, and work as a special education teacher shaped his resistance to the often deficit framings of learning disabilities for his middle school students of color. We conclude with a discussion of the advice Samuel has for current and future special education teachers of color and teacher preparation programs.

Background and History

As a Black, male special education teacher, I (Samuel) can reflect back on several teachers who had a strong impact on my life, especially since I identify with a learning disability and received special education services myself. When I think about what makes a great teacher, and a special education teacher specifically, I think about how the teachers in my life always kept a positive attitude, held high expectations of me, and showed me that they cared about my professional and personal development. The care that these teachers showed me encouraged me to pursue a career as a special education teacher. Navigating my identity as a Black, male in special education was never an easy path, but knowing that my teachers cared about my academic and socio-emotional well-being set a strong foundation for how I approach teaching my own students.

I began my journey into special education as an instructional aide through the Santa Clara County Office of Education. There, I worked with elementary school-aged children with learning disabilities and autism. Through this first experience, I was able to learn about the structures of classroom management and behavior from the teachers I worked with. There were a combination of novice and experienced teachers at this school site, and working alongside them helped me to understand the differences in classroom management approaches that different teachers took toward students with disabilities. In special education, there seemed to be a focus on controlling disabled students' bodies by making them appear more "normal."

After a few years in this placement, I moved into a role in family services. In this position, I worked as an after-school teacher helping with the after-school program providing lunch and indoor/outdoor activities to students with and without disabilities. One thing I noticed right away about the afterschool program was that it wasn't really catered to supporting students with disabilities. For example, there really weren't any modifications or supports for the activities the students were participating in, and it definitely meant that many of the families of children with disabilities couldn't participate as often or as meaningfully as the nondisabled students.

Both of these experiences gave me a clearer understanding of the intricacies, rewards, and challenges involved in working in the field of special education. Learning about how other students in the special education system were being treated and how education wasn't really serving *all* students, I decided that I wanted to go into the field of education. Therefore, I was encouraged to pursue a bachelor's degree in child development after I finished an associate's degree from community college. For me, learning about the development of children was the first step in my education toward becoming a special education teacher. My Bachelor's in Child Development came with information about how to pursue a teaching credential and there was never any doubt for me, as someone with disabilities myself that I would want to work with students with disabilities. Right after my bachelor's degree, I applied for the credential program in special education and, later, the master's program as well.

As a person who identifies with learning disabilities, I received special education services in P-12 schools and had an Individualized Education Plan growing up. The experience in school was really the experience of always trying to, and at times feeling frustrated when I couldn't, be on the same level as my peers. From elementary school, where I was often not allowed to attend the same recess or was placed in smaller classes away from my peers, I always felt embarrassed or left out. It always felt like we (those of us with learning disabilities) were a group of children that were always left behind or treated like second-class citizen students when it came to school events or even applying to college right after high school. The standards in school for a student with disabilities during that time encouraged the majority of us to go to community college, but my plans were different. I really wanted to head to a university after high school but didn't really feel like I had the support or means to do this right after college. Therefore, looking at my options, I chose to attend De Anza Community College, which I thought was one of the best schools to provide me with better services and opportunities for me to build up my academic skills. I also had accommodations throughout college and wanted to use my own experiences to support other students with disabilities. I wanted my students to be able to experience me as a teacher who gave them a positive learning experience and believed in their futures.

Growing up in Santa Clara County, I was able to work in communities and schools near where I grew up. Consequently, some of the same instructional aides who supported me during my schooling as a student in special education were now supporting me as a colleague when I started working as a professional special education teacher.

Knowing the community and the context in which I taught was important to me as an advocate for students with disabilities and for helping my own students with disabilities advocate for themselves. As a special education teacher of color with disabilities, advocating for students with disabilities within my own community became a huge part of my teaching identity.

Challenges of Special Education

There is a level of demoralization that happens when working in special education as part of a school and a district that doesn't seem to care about students with disabilities and students of color. Being a special education teacher is one of the most challenging positions a teacher can take on. I love my students and want them to succeed. Yet, the educational system left me feeling so burnt out. I was overwhelmed by the constant demands associated with maintaining compliance with IEPs that really didn't seem meaningful for my students, and I was rarely provided the time I needed and wanted to catch up and plan for instruction.

This was exacerbated by my experiences of being overlooked and presumed incompetent by my colleagues because of my young age and a belief that I was less knowledgeable because I wasn't teaching in general education. I came into the classroom believing in the power of collaboration, thinking that I could work cooperatively with the other teachers. Maybe we'd have the opportunity to co-teach or work together to design the best instructional program for my students with disabilities. It all seemed so great in my mind, but in reality, my students with disabilities were often placed in the back of the classroom or left out of special events or field trips. This seemed to be a pattern with both me and my students, like neither of us could ever really belong in this space.

On top of the challenges with my colleagues, I also noticed the isolation of being one of the few Black, male teachers with a disability. I think a lot about the intersectionality there and how I am constantly having to think about all of these identities: special educator, Black, disabled. As one of the few Black males at the school site, I sometimes wonder how much of the lack of collaboration and perception of me as less qualified has to do with my race. I sometimes think they underestimate me based on this and perhaps my disability as well. It makes me wonder how I can really advocate for my students with disabilities in a space where neither my students nor I matter. Another significant challenge was the leadership in the school. The administrators were at least as uninformed about disabilities—if not more so—as my colleagues. When my students were being separated or excluded from school activities, the administration never seemed to be able to step in and support them. The lack of support also made me feel like I couldn't win, no matter how hard I advocated for the students. I sometimes think

66　Racism and Ableism in the Classroom and Teacher Education

about quitting or leaving the profession. Maybe becoming an administrator would give me the power I lack as a special education teacher of color because I definitely feel powerless as a teacher.

I don't write all of this to deter anyone from becoming a special education teacher. I *do* have rewarding experiences with my students and love seeing them develop into successful and self-determined individuals. My students and I matter, but the system often makes us feel like we don't. My advocacy won't make much difference if we don't find a way to change the system, regardless of where or how strongly I do it. This is why—in the meantime—I try to emphasize the importance of self-determination with my students and talk to them directly about how ableism plays out in schools and in special education overall and ways for them to navigate their own successful path within a disinterested and often hostile system.

Imposter Syndrome

In Kulkarni et al. (2021), Samuel shared how part of his disabilities included a speech problem and speech delay. He was born premature and did not begin speaking until around the age of four. When he started elementary school, he recalled feeling stressed because of a lack of understanding of the concept of addition and subtraction. There was additional frustration and disappointment at being compared with neurotypical peers who would sometimes get their work displayed on bulletin boards for excelling with the class material. He noted how the whole-class environment made him feel stressed, overwhelmed, and not smart. In this section, we discuss Samuel's feelings of imposter syndrome, particularly when he was in general education settings and wasn't being provided with supports or scaffolds to enhance his educational opportunities.

Recognizing some of his challenges, Samuel's classroom teacher initiated his referral to special education. Initially, his school in East San José offered him a resource classroom placement where he was pulled into smaller group instruction to refine skills in reading, writing, and math. When his family moved closer to South San José, an inclusive special education program recommended as a better option. Samuel spent over an hour on the bus in each direction to get to and from his placement. This new district, unlike East San José, was majority white, and Samuel recalled how he was only one of five Black students there. It was perhaps why the school insisted on keeping him in an inclusive programming environment to reduce stigma and racial tensions related to overrepresentation of Black students in segregated classrooms.

I (Samuel) was always treated differently in school. As a Black, disabled kid, I was often in what was referred to as the "small class." When I moved to a more inclusive setting, it helped me feel like I could be independent. I had the opportunity to construct sentences independently, to read and write more proficiently, and to get involved in art and music. The opportunity to be exposed to art, in particular, felt like an amazing change for me after doubting myself with my academics in school.

As I got older, I learned about the concept of internalized ableism, and how this felt like what I had experienced when I was in smaller special education settings on the East Side of San José. In some ways, I thrived more at the mostly white school I attended in South San José because they had the resources to support my disability. However, it was isolating to feel like I would never see a teacher who looked like me, a Black male role model to look up to. I suppose that was the challenge of never really knowing teachers and other people at school who saw me with all of my different identities (Black and Disabled). It wasn't until I met the sports coach at school that I felt like I had a role model and connection to another Black male.

By the time I started high school, my family had moved me to Fremont where I attended high school. Although I felt like I was better able to adjust socially, I continued to struggle academically, especially in math. My low test scores and appearance were often fodder for my mostly white peers to bully me. I was called "monkey" by these students, without any consequences by the teachers or "Urkel" because I needed to wear glasses. Feeling like an imposter everywhere I went, I began skipping school my freshman year and my already low grades got even worse.

My family transferred me to another high school, where the demographics of students and teachers were a bit more diverse and where the teachers seemed to be more honest with me. This brought up a bit of my confidence and self-esteem, and I began to improve my grades and attendance. Although I continued to be insecure about my academic abilities, I started to see post-secondary education as a possibility. While there was never any real encouragement for me to attend a four-year institution, I believed that I would get there eventually. I started out at community college and worked my way up to my bachelor's and master's degrees at San José State University. Despite having gained entry into a bachelor's and later, a master's program, the imposter syndrome stayed with me. I kept asking myself if I really belonged in college.

It wasn't until I had some positive experiences working in classrooms and taking courses in the special education teacher education program that I started to understand that I had something to offer youth with disabilities. Especially in courses and field experiences where I could draw from my own experiences, I learned that there was value in being able to advocate for my students because I had experienced many of the same things. Not only was I serving my own community—working with students who

68 Racism and Ableism in the Classroom and Teacher Education

looked like me and came in with some of the same academic challenges and imposter syndrome—but also my own confidence was increasing, and my feeling that I didn't belong dissipated. Many of the teachers I worked with in special education identified as white and female, which in some ways helped me to identify myself more proudly as someone who wanted to embrace students' racial identities alongside their disability identities. Sometimes we have to see what not to do to figure out what we want to do.

Navigating Identity

Though students with disabilities are the focus population of special education teachers, less is known about the identities of the teachers themselves. We (Samuel and Saili) wish to share a bit more about the intricacies of working within the special education classroom with intersecting multiply marginalized identities. In the case of Samuel, Black, disabled, and special education teaching identities intersected to inform his experiences.

After graduating from his teacher credential program in special education with both a Mild/Moderate Credential and Master's in Special Education, Samuel continued working as a middle school special education teacher. Intermittently, Samuel also worked with me (Saili) as a research assistant for an affinity space project for special education teachers of color and participated in a series of workshops and learning experiences centered on anti-ableist practices in the classroom. These experiences shifted his approaches to supporting his students. For example, Samuel utilized *direct conversations with his students about disability and ableism.* He shared that he wanted his students to embrace what are often perceived as weaknesses rather than strive to conform to an ableist school structure that didn't value their insight and knowledge. Samuel also championed how direct conversations with students with disabilities would allow them to discover themselves and allow students to self-direct their learning about their identities.

In *Undoing Ableism*, Baglieri and Lalvani (2019) note how ableism exists in schools and our larger society, but that students do not often get opportunities to learn about it.

> Consequently, in school, there are few conversation aimed at addressing children' curiosity about disability and difference. In its place, there is a silence; like the proverbial elephant in the room, the topic of disability remains unmentioned, and the issue of ableism is unaddressed.

Therefore, in Samuel's classroom, there was a need to undo the silence surrounding his students' individual disability identities and address this through dialogue with his students. Specifically, Samuel utilized talking points from Baglieri and Lalvani's (2019) book, which posed questions that asked students where they may have first learned about disability, for them to define disability for themselves, and then to connect the identity of disability to themselves. Students did this in multiple ways: by sharing stories, drawings, poetry, and music. As a student with learning disabilities himself, Samuel understood that there was no one right way of demonstrating knowledge. He shared, for example, how, as a teacher education student, he did not feel confident in his written abilities but was more comfortable sharing visual or audio representations of his thinking and appreciated when his professors had these kinds of opportunities for him. Understanding the importance of multiple means of representation and expression from universal design for learning, Samuel was able to incorporate this strategy into helping his students understand disability and how it connected with ableism in schools and society. He also helped students to learn how disability identity was one of the many identities his middle school students held.

In special education, as Baglieri and Lalvani (2019) pointed out, disability is thought of as an "elephant in the room," and students are rarely given an opportunity to learn about the impacts of this identity on their own learning and development. In part because of compliance issues related to the Individualized Education Plan and specific student services and supports, there has often been a fear of disclosure related to students with disabilities (Voulgarides, 2018). While confidentiality is important, in some cases, students with disabilities are being denied access to their identities. By taking the workshops as part of our research study on disability-centered culturally sustaining practices (Kulkarni et al., 2023), Samuel and other teachers like him learned from the voices and experiences of multiply marginalized disabled people of color and utilized their methods and materials to supplement his instructional practices with his own students.

Principle Two of Disability-Centered, Culturally Sustaining Pedagogies (DCCSPs; Kulkarni et al., 2023) states that we must privilege the lived experiences of multiply marginalized disabled people of color and youth. Samuel employed this framework in his classroom by moving from helping his students recognize their identities as disabled, and as people of color, to using these identities to inform his teaching and curriculum. Specifically, Samuel encouraged his students to generate reading and language arts assignments that tapped into their own experiences as disabled youth of color. In other words, *the curriculum was centered around disabled youth of color.*

Samuel utilized poetry, music, and artwork to help students showcase their identities. For example, the eighth-grade curriculum calls for students

70 Racism and Ableism in the Classroom and Teacher Education

to be able to demonstrate an understanding of figurative and connotative meanings in the English language. In Samuel's class, students were able to compose poems about their lived experiences that incorporated a series of these different types of meanings and then take turns reading the poems in class. The students would then be able to learn about their peers while simultaneously trying to figure out some of the hidden meanings shared in the poem. Discussing disability specifically in their poems was another way that helped the students feel connected to their disability as an identity.

After students began to recognize their identities and connect more deeply with them through the curriculum, Samuel also started to encourage students to begin to *self-monitor their academic progress* in class and, in some cases, during their IEP meetings. The process of self-monitoring and, in many cases, self-determining their learning goals, helped Samuel and his students to challenge the existing system of special education in which goals are provided *for* students rather than *with* them. Learning to self-monitor their goals and development were difficult skills for students to master at first, but eventually they began to feel confident. This skill also enabled students to know when to self-advocate for additional support from Samuel and other teachers. When students faced a challenge or conflict, Samuel could rely on his students to come to him directly with any issues. This built a trusting relationship between him and his students. Table 4.1 summarizes some of the practices that Samuel incorporated to help his students shape their own intersectional identities.

As seen in the table above, Samuel's use of various strategies and supports to engage his students at the intersections of race and ability. By helping students see themselves in their curriculum, providing them decision-making power in their learning goals and progress, and sharing his identities with his students (which then allowed them to see themselves in their teacher), Samuel cultivated a strong sense of identity for his students.

Sample Lesson Plan

I (Samuel) wanted to share a sample lesson plan I created that illustrates the kinds of content and supports I want to present to my students. I was part of a program from the National Endowment for the Humanities on Desegregation in Education. As part of the program, I learned some important historical knowledge and used that to help my students to understand some of the disadvantages of the implementation of the 1954 Brown vs. Board of Education court decision to integrate schools. We looked at some of the massive resistances to Brown vs. Board and some of the challenges related to busing Black students over an hour a day to attend school. We also talked about the parallels between this and some of the segregation we

TABLE 4.1 Summary of Connection and Reframed Identity Practices

Practice	Description	Reframing	Example
Lack of discussion about students' disability due to compliance and confidentiality concerns.	Concerns over confidentiality with the IEP and disclosure of disability are often drivers in keeping teachers from discussing disability more directly with their students. Even without the risk of disclosure, helping students understand and process their own disabilities tends to be limited in special education.	Instead, Samuel utilized direct conversations with his students about their learning disabilities. Along with sharing about his own experiences being labeled with disabilities and the process of going through special education himself, Samuel encouraged his students to learn about their disabilities as a way to help them learn advocacy and improve their overall self-perceptions and understanding of their identities.	Samuel's class incorporated opportunities for students to share their stories of disability individually and, if they felt comfortable, with their peers. Stories incorporated their lived experiences as told through written narratives, poetry, music, artwork, and voice recordings. Students were given choices as to how they wanted to share their stories.
Lack of representation of disability and ableism in the classroom.	Students at Samuel's school site did not have access to curriculum that centered their experiences as learning disabled. Additionally, when books on disability were available, they were often limited to white, disabled students. Drawing from DCCSPs and his time working with disabled community scholars of color, Samuel was able to incorporate more intersectional disability materials and curriculum into his class.	Students have access to disability-centered curriculum and characters/stories that center multiply marginalized disabled youth of color. Samuel reframes the curriculum to add more intersectional narratives created by disabled community scholars of color.	Samuel adds readings and other materials to his classroom curriculum, such as poetry and readings from Lydia XZ Brown, Leroy F. Moore Jr., and Poor Press, which engages youth through accessible educational materials on concepts such as ableism, intersections of racism and ableism, and poverty scholarship.

(*Continued*)

TABLE 4.1 (Continued)

Practice	Description	Reframing	Example
Students are separated from many of the decisions that directly impact their learning and progress, such as IEP meetings, decisions regarding classroom management and expectations, and overall hopes and dreams.	Students at Samuel's school site did not have opportunities to attend their own IEP meetings, make decisions about their own behavior and academic progress, and share their overall hopes and dreams for their future. Oftentimes, students were thought of as incapable of having this kind of autonomy or self-determination.	Samuel reframed his classroom so that his multiply marginalized students with learning disabilities would be able to make decisions about their own lives. He introduced concepts of self-advocacy and self-determination.	Students in Samuel's class were encouraged to attend their own IEP meetings and planning procedures for these meetings. Samuel supported students in making plans for sharing in their meetings and helped students to advocate for their own needs. In conjunction with learning about their disabilities, Samuel helped students to understand what kinds of supports or services might be beneficial to them as they move through middle school, high school, and eventually graduate.

continue to see in schools today related to special education and how being Black and Brown with a disability can mean having less access to inclusion. I asked students to draw upon their real-life experiences and, through role play, to discuss inequities related to racism and ableism in the United States. We also talked about how integration impacts students' sense of self, belonging, and identity. What might it have been like to have been one of only a few Black students in an all-white school? How does a student's identity get shaped by being in a segregated classroom with only other students with disabilities who are Black and Brown? These are some of the things I tried to get my students to reflect on in this lesson (see Figure 4.1).

NATIONAL ENDOWMENT FOR THE HUMANITIES

2021 NEH Lesson Plan

Do students of color feel they belong in schools in California following Brown vs. Board of Education Decision?

Name: Samuel Bland

School or Institution: Aptitud Academy

Projected Date for Implementation: October 2021

Title of Lesson	*Color Students Sense of Belonging in Education*
Overview	*The lesson will consist of investigation of historical education disadvantages from the past about the untold stories of how African Americans and predominantly black civil rights organizations worked to implement the Supreme Court's decision after 1954 in **Virginia and California**. Students will be able to explore the disadvantages of black students in the education climate from the civil rights movement from 1954-1965 related to the **implementation of Brown vs. Board of Education.** Students will be able to share their own learning through visual boards through **digital or paper/pencil creations.** Last, students will use their own action to implement their own ideas of how schools are better or worse through open letters to city officials.*
Essential or Investigative Question	1. *Could you share the similarities and differences of schools and communities racial makeup in your surrounding neighborhood to Brown vs. Board of Education?* 2. *What do you notice about the economic status of your neighborhood that are similar and different from neighborhoods you have visited?* 3. *How are you able to relate to other students based on the same ethnic background, family connections, or common beliefs about desegregation in schools?* 4. *Which tactic would you use to enforce desegregation related to the outcome of the Brown vs. Board of Education?* **(Examples: sit ins, marching, write letters to government officials)**
Audience	• This activity is best suited for educators of the following grade levels • Grades 6-8 **This activity is best suited for educators of the following content areas** • *Social Studies/ Social Sciences*

FIGURE 4.1 NEH Lesson Plan

NATIONAL ENDOWMENT FOR THE HUMANITIES

Time Required	The lesson will have a targeted time of 50 minutes of 1 class period for a five week lesson plan.
Goal	1. Students will be able to identify the geographic makeup of their community related to neighborhood, community, and especially schools. 2. Students will be able use inquiring skills related to racial tensions and injustices from the reformation of schooling. 3. Students will be able to showcase using primary sources about segregation through public policy **(Amendments) (Constitution)** of having a free public and equal opportunity in schooling. **(Display the Amendments from primary source).**
Standards	2A: Include accurate information based on current and confirmed research. 2E: Promote self and collective empowerment; 2G: Encourage cultural understanding of how different groups have struggled and worked together, highlighting core ethnic studies concepts such as equality, justice, race, ethnicity, indigeneity, etc.
Objectives	By the end of this lesson, students are able to: • SWBA cites accurate information from confirmed research. • SWBA to promote self and collective empowerment through personal connections through shared experiences. • SWBA encourages cultural understanding about different groups struggling with race equity in school trajectory.
Classroom Materials	1. Projector (Smart Board) 2. Poster Board (Display Boards) or (Jamboard) 3. Scissors 4. Markers 5. Glue 6. Computer (WIFI) 7. Voice Recorder (Phone, Digital, or Computer)

FIGURE 4.1 (Continued)

Drawing from my (Samuel's) own experiences as never really seeing myself in my teachers until I met one of the sports coaches, and also never really seeing disability being talked about when I was in school, I decided that my students deserved better opportunities to learn about their disabilities and use that information to become strong self-advocates for themselves after high school and into their lives. Additionally, having access to books and materials that centered intersectional disability gave students more opportunities for connection and meaning. Learning about all of the

NATIONAL ENDOWMENT FOR THE HUMANITIES

Background	Students will draw on their experiences about their own point of view of what schooling means to them and what they have seen in relation to teachers, peers, and other staff members through classroom treatment.
Procedure	1. Students will watch two videos **May 17 1954, Brown vs Education and Voices of History: Sylvia Mendez**. Then, Students will read an Interactive PowerPoint and Discussions **Keep on Keeping On; Brian J. Daugherity** (Students will use voice recording or type their response about the interactive reading from the powerpoint into the Seesaw assignment). (Day 1) 2. Review of Reading: Research **(Pedagogy Discussion about Reading) (Day 2)** 3. Start College Board (Images of Civil Rights (Brown vs. Education, Court Rulings, Protests) (Written Expression Bullet Points of descriptive analysis about the implementation. (Day 2) 4. Continue with Collage Board: (Day 3) 5. Presentation of Collage Board (Day 4) 6. Letter to City Officials (Day 5)
Differentiation (Optional)	Provide students to use Google documents to speak to text features for struggling writers and readers. Provide students the option to create jam boards instead of poster boards who are challenged with gross motor skills. Provide intensive 1 to 1 or small groups to support in research to find credible sources.
Assessment	The checklist of components/expectations will be used to evaluate student's outcomes of learning and meeting expectations.
Take Informed Action	Students will draw on real life experiences after their presentation through stories or role play about the inequities or ableism that has shaped racism to segregate the school system in the United States. **Student Action Plan**: Students will write anonymous letters about school desegregation (redlining) to use their voices of what type of resources (playgrounds, equipment, textbooks, reading books) or even the type of staff to make education meaningful. These letters will be sent to the **City officials of San Jose** to hear the voices of students from a Title 1 school who need the same resources from the other well funded school to receive the same equitable and opportunities to succeed in the classroom.
Collaboration	I would ask students to record conversations with their parents or someone close to them about their own school experience growing up to showcase the benefits and drawbacks in order for students to be able to use the information when having whole class discussions. **(Oral Recordings)**
Reflection	When receiving feedback, I was really looking for opportunities to improve the delivery and for the lesson to be connected to the student backgrounds of Mexican descent. Through the feedback, I thought of a great way with the strong message related to litigation during the Civil Rights Movement, I thought it would be helpful for students to write letters to city officials to know that regardless of age everyone has a voice. I was able to pose open-ended questions for students to have stake in the conversations surrounded around segregation and race in the classroom.

FIGURE 4.1   (Continued)

important work that the community scholars who wrote the books, poetry, and other resources did helped my students to see their own potential. For example, I have a couple of students who never thought that they could go to college, and then they got to look at Leroy F. Moore's book *Black Disabled Art History 101*, and I told them about how Leroy is getting a

76 Racism and Ableism in the Classroom and Teacher Education

master's degree and a doctorate. This opened up some meaningful possibilities for them.

Although there were some challenges with families getting on the same page around sharing information on student disabilities with them, eventually almost all of them saw the benefits with their kids. Teaching my students self-advocacy skills has been a really great way to help them understand some of their own struggles and how they might need to share that information with their other teachers when they are frustrated or don't understand things from class. It's also been a great way for them to develop an identity around their disability and learn to be more accepting of their learning differences. Some of my students have been channeling their thoughts about their disabilities into additional narratives or poetry to express themselves, and it's been a really cool process to watch this transformation.

Conclusion

Abernathy and Taylor (2009) found that there is a strong need for teacher education to provide encouragement and support for teachers to talk to students about their disabilities. They noted that while there seemed to be a great deal of effort related to helping other teachers and educational professionals learn about a student's disability and ways to support their progress, less attention is being paid to how to address this topic with the students themselves and developing a specific plan in conjunction with students to support this knowledge. Older studies have also shown that knowing about one's disability in secondary educational settings is a great way for students to become self-advocates in post-secondary educational settings (Byron, 1990; Dalke, 1993). McLean (2008) also notes how it is an ethical responsibility to teach young adults about their disability as a way to change "ableist and oppressive views of disability" (p. 605).

Samuel, therefore, helped shape the identities of his multiply marginalized students of color with disabilities and enabled them to develop positive self-concepts in special education. This is often a difficult undertaking given the focus of special education on moving students with disabilities toward achieving status as "normal" (Kenny & Shevlin, 2001). Through a combination of allowing students to develop self-advocacy and self-determination, utilizing books and materials produced by the disabled community to provide examples of representation, and encouraging students to attend their own Individualized Education Plan meetings (and in some cases leading them), Samuel has provided his students with empowerment, ownership, and a strong sense of identity.

It took me (Samuel) a long time to come to an acceptance of my identity as having a disability. I always felt more comfortable with my identity as a Black man, but in our community disability was sometimes taboo. I was lucky that my parents supported my learning, and that's why I had the opportunities to move around so much growing up and was able to find school placements where I could start to make progress academically. Despite their support, however, I learned that teachers—specifically teachers of color—really matter when it comes to being in special education. I had so few of these teachers growing up, and it was really hard to see myself in my teachers and my learning.

Once I developed my sense of self as a Black, disabled man, and was able to learn to accept this as part of my identity, I felt like I was able to become a better special education teacher to my students. I began to understand a bit more about the imposter syndrome I felt during high school and college, and channel those perceptions of not feeling like I was good enough into telling my story to anyone who would listen. I wrote a book chapter with Dr. K (Saili) and another teacher of color (Joanna), who first shared my story of having a disability. I learned how important it is to share my story with my students and then encourage them to come to terms with their own identities through their stories. Our classroom has become a more dynamic space since the students and I started being more open about our identities, and I feel like it will set them up for success to be proud of who they are and to advocate for what they need. Knowing our own identities as teachers of color in special education is so important and helps us to impart this knowledge to our students.

In this chapter, we (Saili and Samuel) drew from Erikson's (1968) theory of psychosocial development to highlight some of the past, present, and future experiences that Samuel had that led to his identity development as a Black, male special education teacher. Samuel used this identity to then develop critical practices in his special education classroom that supported his multiply marginalized disabled students of color. Generating his identity as a special education teacher of color led to transformative practices in Samuel's classroom. This work, however, is not always valued by administrators or the systems of special education and schools, which are often performance-based (Wamba, 2021).

The challenges that Samuel shared initially related to being a special education teacher in a racist/ableist school system are real and significant. Navigating some of these systems as a special education teacher of color is not always safe, especially when these teachers are openly discussing race and disability in the classroom. Specifically, teachers who are defying more traditional conceptions of disability and special education are often socially

78 Racism and Ableism in the Classroom and Teacher Education

ostracized and risk reprimand or termination (Duncan-Andrade, 2009). After our conversations for this chapter, Samuel tried working in schools in the state of Washington as a special education teacher but faced some of the same challenges and frustrations he noted in California schools. Therefore, he decided that he would leave teaching and continue to advocate for disability rights and justice by sharing his stories as a special education teacher of color in alternative ways.

Samuel is currently working in the field of transportation and hospitality, both of which, he shares, allow him to continue his advocacy work with disability by supporting the community rather than school-aged students. This is important to note as special education can often be an emotionally traumatic space for special education teachers of color, especially those who are trying to negotiate district-wide mandates and performance outcomes against generating a curriculum and content that are identity-focused for their students. Leaving special education was a difficult decision for Samuel, but ultimately one that allowed him to continue to incorporate anti-racist and anti-ableist practices more broadly. He shared that he has not necessarily left teaching behind forever, but some of the issues around building resistance with his students were not always deemed a priority by his administrative staff, and that—coupled with the isolation of being one of the few teachers of color—drove him out of special education and teaching, at least temporarily.

Regardless of what I (Samuel) decide to do in the future, however, whether it's teaching or continuing to work in hospitality, I believe that being a teacher really helped me to come to terms with my own disability and hopefully did the same for the students that I worked with. I think it's so important that we continue to have a strong sense of self and identity in whatever work we end up doing, especially where ableism is concerned, and this is just another way we fight back!

References

Abernathy, T. V., & Taylor, S. S. (2009). Teacher perceptions of students' understanding of their own disability. *Teacher Education and Special Education, 32*(2), 121–136.

Baglieri, S., & Lalvani, P. (2019). *Undoing ableism: Teaching about disability in K-12 classrooms.* Routledge.

Byron, J. (1990, July). *Paper (untitled) presented at the 1990 conference on post-secondary issues for LD students, Hartfield, CT.* ldx.sagepub.com/cgi/content/refs/27/7/413

Dalke, C. (1993). Making a successful transition from high school to college: A model program. In S. A. Vogel & P. B. Adelman (Eds.), *Success for college students with disabilities* (pp. 57–80). Springer-Verlag.

Duncan-Andrade, J. (2009). Note to educators: Hope required when growing roses in concrete. *Harvard Educational Review, 79*(2), 181–194.

Erikson, E. H. (1968). *Identity: Youth and crisis.* Norton.

Forber-Pratt, A. J., Lyew, D. A., Mueller, C., & Samples, L. B. (2017). Disability identity development: A systematic review of the literature. *Rehabilitation Psychology, 62*(2), 198.

Gallchóir, C. Ó., O'Flaherty, J., & Hinchion, C. (2018). Identity development: What I notice about myself as a teacher. *European Journal of Teacher Education, 41*(2), 138–156. https://doi.org/10.1080/02619768.2017.1416087

Kenny, M., & Shevlin, M. (2001). Normality and power: Desire and reality for students with disabilities in mainstream schools. *Irish Journal of Sociology, 10*(2), 105–119.

Kulkarni, S., Bland, S., & Gaeta, J. M. (2021). In our own words: Special education teachers of color with dis/abilities. In C. A. O'Brien, W. R. Black, & A. B. Danzig (Eds.), *Who decides: Power, disability and educational leadership.* IAP.

Kulkarni, S. S., Bland, S., & Gaeta, J. M. (2022). From support to action: A critical affinity group of special education teachers of color. *Teacher Education and Special Education, 45*(1), 43–60.

Kulkarni, S. S., Miller, A. L., Nusbaum, E. A., Pearson, H., & Brown, L. X. (2023). Toward disability-centered, culturally sustaining pedagogies in teacher education. Critical Studies in Education, 2, 1–21.

McLean, M. A. (2008). Teaching about disability: An ethical responsibility? *International Journal of Inclusive Education, 12*(5–6), 605–619.

Moore, L. (2017). *Black disabled art history 101.* Xochitl Justice Press.

Roberts, C. A. (2013). *Identity development of literacy teachers of adolescents with significant cognitive disabilities* [Doctoral Dissertation, The University of Wisconsin-Madison].

Voulgarides, C. (2018). *Does compliance matter in special education?: IDEA and the hidden inequities of practice.* Teachers College Press.

Wamba, N. (2021). School leadership in the era of neoliberalism. *Psychology & Its Contexts/Psychologie a Její Kontexty, 12*(2), 23–38.

5

JOANNA

Multiply Marginalized Disabled Students' Discipline Disparities in Middle School

With Contributions by Joanna De Leon Gaeta

We start this chapter with a prayer. Ground your feet on mama earth, however it works for you and close your eyes. Take in a deep breath. Thank you Creator(s) for another day in life. Appreciations for the relatives of First Nations of people whose land we're sitting, standing, wheeling, lying, dreaming and visioning upon. We thank you for taking care of mama earth through the genocide, violence, colonization, removal and for being here with us 530 years later, walking with us in liberation. Prayers to all the Black, Brown, Poor, Indigenous and Disabled relatives who die on the streets due to homelessness, ableism and racism and all the ways the system actually kills these human bodies. We pray for change . . . for you . . . for us . . . for all of us.

—Tiny Gray-Garcia, *Poor Magazine/Press*

We begin this chapter with words from Tiny Gray-Garcia, founder of Poor Magazine and Poor Press, in order to ground us in the seriousness of the issues we plan to discuss. As Tiny shares, systems of ableism and racism can result in the actual death of Black and Brown people (Meiners & Winn, 2012), and we draw from schools, as one of these systems, that can significantly alter the trajectories of young people's lives. In particular, we want to focus on how the structures of discipline in schools can impact young disabled students of color and can implicate them in the school-to-prison nexus (Meiners & Winn, 2012). Meiners and Winn (2012) state how part of our challenges includes how to build decarceration initiatives and methods to make schools and communities safer. She argues that this must be done by augmenting (and we'd add eradicating) the carceral state in which

DOI: 10.4324/9781003653783-6

the system of education operates. Joanna's experiences as a student of color with acquired health issues and as someone who has faced houselessness make her observations and instructional decisions as a special education teacher of color particularly insightful. She starts by sharing how she became a special education teacher and then provides key observations about how her mostly male students of color experienced middle school and disciplinary actions.

Background

I (Joanna) come into the field of special education as a person who has experienced homelessness, poverty, abuse, and disease. These experiences inform the way I approach life, my work with my students in the classroom, and my religious beliefs. The most challenging time in my life growing up was when I was in middle school. During that period, my parents enrolled me in school band, which became a positive outlet for me, along with sports. A teacher who left a mark on me at that time was Ms. Tenant. She was a woman of Dutch descent and just over four feet tall. Ms. Tenant's classroom felt safe because it held students to clear expectations and fostered a warm, supportive environment when everything else seemed so chaotic for me. It was very predictable, unlike my life at home. My parents were struggling in their marriage, and we were still living in a shelter. My father was abusive toward my mother and would act out in aggressive ways. For these reasons, school became an escape from the chaos at home. School felt like a sanctuary.

Ironically enough, despite the chaos and abuse at home, my family and I attended church regularly. Being involved in the school band, I also became involved in the church's music ministry. This is where my faith and education connect. At the time, I was assisting the youth worship team by teaching different youth how to play musical instruments and how to play a worship set. Some of the youth (ages 11–16) I was teaching music to would bring their homework and try to complete it before the day was done. Though I would not necessarily call myself a tutor, because it was not an official role, I always arrived at the church early and stayed late so that the youth would be able to count on me for this support. Many of the youth had parents who were in and out of rehabilitation programs. The rehabilitation programs were to escape gang life, provide reform opportunities for convicted felons, provide addiction support for drugs and/or alcohol, and provide opportunities to escape domestic abuse and/or prostitution. Many of the youth shared how difficult it was to concentrate on school and homework when there was so much emotional and/or physical trauma happening in their homes. Supporting these youth increased my own awareness of how school and home could be so disconnected. For example, how does a student worry about fractions when they're worried about food? This juxtaposition of home and school motivated me to pursue a career in education and to be someone who could support youth in navigating these types of trauma in their lives. Going forward, I share a little bit about that first position I held as a middle school special education teacher and the disparities I saw my Black and Brown male minority students experience as students of color and students with disabilities. I also talk about how I continue to advocate for Black and Brown students with disabilities, despite all of the systemwide challenges with administration and the way we treat discipline for this group of students.

Another reason I decided to go into teaching was related to my own experiences of emotional and mental health in middle school. I was often depressed and experienced emotional trauma due to the fact that my family's housing situation was insecure during that time. My family moved in and out of homeless shelters and ended up in a trailer park where four of us shared a two-bedroom, forty-seven-foot camper. During the winter, our camper did not have the best heating, and during the summers, it used to get too hot to sleep indoors. Financially, this was all my family could afford, and the stress of housing insecurity often led to me being defiant with my teachers or engaging in self-injurious behaviors. These stresses led to cycles of abuse between my parents and also between them and their children: with myself being one of the recipients of that abuse. At the same time, despite some of the struggles I faced during middle school, I also considered school a safe haven. My mother always talked about education being an opportunity. As a high schooler, I realized that with school being my haven, it would also be my way to safety—it would be my way out of abuse and the cycle of generational trauma. Due to systemic injustices that my Latino family faced, school provided things such as structure, food, warmth, and a sense of security that was not available at home.

The teachers who supported me helped me to find a way to navigate the requirements of school despite all of the emotional trauma I was facing at home. Their support helped me earn a spot at the University of California, Santa Cruz, where I did my undergraduate program in literature and education. One of the courses that I remember required us to spend time working at a school site. Although I requested and desired to work with middle school students based on my prior experiences with the youth at my church, the university placed me in a 5th- and 6th-grade classroom. When I got to the site, the teacher directed me to support the students with disabilities in the classroom. This was my first experience working alongside students with disabilities in school. Because these experiences were so positive, I decided to apply to be an instructional assistant when I graduated from college.

Aside from my mandatory volunteer hours for the fieldwork course, I had not had any other opportunities to work in a classroom setting, and I recognized that the instructional aide position might provide me with some additional experiences that would help me decide on a career path. Fortunately, I was given a position to support a middle school special education classroom for students with mild to moderate disabilities.

The classroom teacher at that site became a mentor to me and supported me in navigating the process of earning my credential in special education. She guided me in taking the required qualifying examinations for California, such as the California Basic Education Skills Test (CBEST), the California Subject-Matter Education Test (CSET), and the Reading Instruction California Assessment (RICA). Additionally, this mentor teacher supported my application to a special education credential program at San José State University and advocated for me to teach alongside her classroom (a veteran teacher was retiring, and she put in a good word for me to that school principal). I was her instructional assistant for about two years but had never really considered becoming a full-time special education teacher until having had her support. Therefore, I became a credential candidate at San José State University and simultaneously an intern candidate (the lead classroom teacher for the middle school classroom while taking courses for my credential).

Challenges With Special Education

As teachers, we realize that challenges present themselves each year. That can manifest if there's a change of administration, if school borders change, if there are school closures, or if teachers are moved to different sites. Before teaching alongside my teacher mentor at what we will call School A, I accepted an immediate opening at a sister middle school in our district (this will be School B). One of the areas that presented a big challenge for me in special education was the lack of mentorship at School B. While I was grateful to the teacher who helped bring me into this field, I noticed that once I started working full-time and independently, I did not have that same level of support at School B. Accepting this position at this new school left me feeling distanced from my mentor teacher and not being supported by the administration. At School A, I also had gotten to know the support staff in the classroom. They were knowledgeable about the students and helped me to adjust or learn about how to best provide support. Unfortunately, School B did not have this resource. Most of the support staff were new along with me. We struggled to learn about the students while also

84 Racism and Ableism in the Classroom and Teacher Education

navigating overdue Individualized Education Plans (IEPs) and compliance with implementing services and administering academic assessments.

During this year, we also participated in an audit from the California Department of Education. I remember being interviewed about student accommodations, goals, number of services, and assessments. At the time, it felt like I was in the hot seat, being interrogated by officials who were doing their due diligence when it came to IEP compliance. I was still learning but not comfortable with the assessment process and the IEP writing process. And while I worked with great teachers at this site, our caseloads were overloaded, and we were simply trying to survive. I didn't learn how to properly assess students until my second year as a teacher (when I transferred back to School A). Working as a special education teacher while also obtaining a credential meant that I was being asked to assess students and complete IEPs before I had been properly given the tools to help with these tasks. Overall, my challenges boiled down to support for me. I felt like my support system at School A was not adequately matched at School B and I was left to figure things out at the expense of my students, who needed me and deserved better.

Behavioral Observations and Challenges

As things started to change and I became more familiar with my classroom and my new role as the lead teacher, I began to notice several significant patterns among my students. It was clear to me that the Black and Brown students and male students seemed to always make up almost the entire caseload for me and other special education teachers at the school site. I could always count the number of female students on my caseload on one hand. This overrepresentation of Black and Brown male students in special education made an impression on me. Black and Brown male students overrepresentation in casework had important implications for the students and their middle school experiences.

From the beginning, I noticed the imbalance of service. When I started at both School A and School B, I observed that Black and Brown males were being heavily excluded and segregated from school settings for *any* behavioral challenges. In some instances, these behaviors were similar to those I saw from students in general education classrooms, yet only the students with disabilities were being heavily segregated from their peers. Many times, I wondered if this disparity was taking place because some students with disabilities were unable to communicate the sequence of events in a cohesive manner as opposed to their general education peers. As a resource specialist, my role was supposed to supplement the general education classroom by providing supports in reading and math for students with learning disabilities yet oftentimes I noted how teachers would just send out students on my caseload as if they took too many redirections or had outbursts that weren't neurotypical (i.e., lasted longer or required more support) and could be due to their disability.

When I started my master's program at San José State University, I wanted to spend time capturing some of what I observed about these disparities. I was one of the few students in the special education program who decided to do a qualitative study using a process where I interviewed students and reviewed artifacts related to their behaviors. One of my students, for example, spoke about the guilt he felt throughout his entire body due to the responses to his "bad" behavior. Consequences for this behavior often meant that he couldn't participate in recess or other activities with his peers. He also spoke about how he experienced fear of not doing the "right thing" because it always meant the principal's office or being kept inside.

Another thing I noticed was how much miscommunication there was between school leadership and teachers at my school. For example, one of my students got suspended for calling out in class or "acting up." When he didn't show up for school the next day, the administration office called his home to see whether he had ditched class, despite the fact he had already been suspended. These kinds of miscommunications were common for my Black and Brown students with disabilities and led to some of them to feel like this school was not really there for them or had their best interest in mind. This same student also shared how the teachers would call him out in front of the whole class when he misbehaved, which led to a lot of anger and humiliation.

Additionally, when I reviewed behavioral artifacts such as suspension notices and data related to suspensions and expulsions for the school online, I noticed that several students had multiple referrals, but often only one call home to the parents or guardians was noted. For one of my students, there were like 19 referrals and only one call home. What happened to the other 18 times he was in trouble? Why weren't his parents informed? The opportunity to include these situations as part of my master's thesis really opened my eyes to the complexity of some of the disparities that I was seeing among my students. Were there challenges with their behaviors in school and in my classes? Absolutely! But I came to realize how those challenges were often associated with how the school system treated them like bad kids or, in some instances, like criminals.

Through my observations and work with male minority students, I saw some of the direct links between discipline and ableism. In middle school, there were often challenges with navigating student behavior in general. When students got into a fight in general education, however, I noted how students on my caseload would receive harsher punishments than the

86 Racism and Ableism in the Classroom and Teacher Education

general education students. For example, during a classroom fight between several students, my student, a Black male with a learning disability, received a five-day, out-of-school suspension while his peer in general education got a two-day, in-house suspension. Both were equal contributors to the issue, but the administration punished my student more severely.

Discipline Disparities Among Male Minority Students

What Joanna's thesis and personal story above revealed is that Black and Brown students in her middle school special education classroom were often subjected to harsher discipline practices that lowered their sense of trust and belonging in school (Carter et al., 2017). As Carter et al. (2017) explain, "racial and ethnic stereotypes are deep rooted in our history; among these the dangerous Black male stereotype is especially relevant" (p. 207). A national analysis of data from Gage et al. (2019) indicates that approximately 23% of Black students with a disability received some form of suspension as compared to 9% of Hispanic and white students and 6% of Asian students. Much of what Joanna observed and captured through her action-research study affirms these statistics with qualitative data that highlights how racism and ableism cooperate in schools to further marginalize students of color with disabilities.

Prior studies have found that simply incorporating interventions and practices in isolation from a deep understanding of the systemic issues involved in discipline do not have lasting, or meaningful, impacts (Kulkarni et al., 2024). Joanna shared that she needed to understand how racism and ableism operated in schools in order to design meaningful ways for students to feel welcome and heard in her classroom. To help her think about making changes to her curriculum and her instructional practices and advocacy for her students, Joanna participated in professional development experiences, including our workshops led by disabled community activists. Though Joanna knew that real change requires leadership shifts and broader commitments by those at the school site, professional development opportunities equipped her with skills that could help her students feel like they could trust and rely on her to support them while they were in this harmful environment. Below, Joanna details two key areas of transition that support her students using a humanizing approach rather than a punitive approach.

Humanizing Practices for Male Minority Students

Joanna's practice of making students feel whole in the classroom started by allowing students to share their stories and experiences in authentic ways. She did this through the practice of *educational journey mapping* with students. Annamma (2016) shares how educational journey mapping allows for the interrogation of space between individuals and social structures and creates a link between individuals' experiences with issues of racism and ableism along with the systemic structures that generate these traumatic experiences. Although Joanna was unable to incorporate these experiences into her action research study when involved in observations with her male minority students, she was able to incorporate journey mapping as a practice into her classroom to allow her students to more authentically share their experiences. Journey mapping information, then, can be used to present to leadership in order to activate policy changes that support students' sense of belonging (Annamma, 2016). While Joanna was not able to immediately change the school culture, which included plenty of suspensions that targeted students of color and students with disabilities, she used her observations and student interactions to spotlight these inequities for her administration, which can begin the conversations around change.

Another way that Joanna was able to begin to shift some of the discipline disparities she observed in her practices was through encouraging students to communicate their needs directly with teachers and staff. Many of her students struggled with executive functioning and learning disabilities. Creating *healthy opportunities for communication* in the classroom has become critical to undoing harmful structures within school. Joanna does this by providing a variety of communication options for her students. For example, some students have difficulty verbalizing their needs.

I (Joanna) tend to have students communicate through their writing. We keep active communication logs or journals as a way for the student and I to share personal information about their progress on their IEP goals and their overall needs in this way. This allows students to express things they wouldn't otherwise be able to share in our class. For students who have trouble writing down their thoughts, I allow them to share verbally or to draw pictures to communicate. We're fortunate that our school got a nice set of Chromebooks so students can also use graphic design and computer-generated visuals to help them communicate with me as well. It's a balance between using the computer for games and for communication, but overall, the Chromebook has been a positive tool for communication for my students.

One other way we've been able to use visuals to communicate our goals for the year is through the use of vision boards. My students have used vision boards as a way to communicate their hopes for the future, their visions for themselves for the year, and some lightness and joy. In Figures 5.1 and 5.2, you can see two examples of my students' vision boards. In Figure 5.1, one of my students pastes the beginning of the word "make happen" and

88 Racism and Ableism in the Classroom and Teacher Education

FIGURE 5.1 Student Vision Board Creation Example

has the word "believe" on his board. This shows how we emphasize positive communication and motivation for the start of a new school year. In Figure 5.2, another student's vision board for motivation includes positive associations such as "energy" and "make 'em laugh." Overall, this exercise was an opportunity for us to focus on positive communication and help students to map out their goals in a supportive environment.

Conclusion

In Cruz et al. (2021), we note how deficit ideologies are realized through the lens of schooling and how this particularly impacts multiply marginalized youth with disabilities. As Artiles and Jacks (n.d.) note, how teachers interpret students' behavior has a direct impact on how they perceive and

FIGURE 5.2 Student Vision Board Creation Example

enact consequences for those behaviors. What is considered to be appropriate behavior is also directly tied to whiteness and dominant ideologies of participation in school (Cruz et al., 2021). As Joanna shared, her students felt the direct impacts of the decisions and consequences of their behavior through exclusionary forms of discipline. These forms of exclusion dehumanized her students and made them feel as though they did not belong in school. The deficit ways in which her students were framed and how this

90 Racism and Ableism in the Classroom and Teacher Education

TABLE 5.1 Summary of Connection and Belonging Practices

Practice	Description	Reframing	Example
Few opportunities to engage and create a sense of belonging for students who are deemed as troublemakers in school.	Students who engage in what are deemed as problematic behaviors are often provided direct consequences. In the case of students of color with disabilities, these consequences often lead to segregation or separation from their peers in general education.	Instead, Joanna uses educational journey mapping to allow students to share the impacts of discipline on their overall self-concept and sense of belonging in school. Students also get to paint a more complex picture of who they are, which was previously reduced to their problematic behavior.	Joanna used educational journey mapping to complicate the overly simplistic picture of her students of color with disabilities and their behaviors. By focusing on the impact of discipline and their overall journeys through education, students felt more connected to school. Eventually, Joanna can provide this information to the leadership team to help reframe the existing narratives of her students and the negative impacts of exclusionary discipline.
Few opportunities for students to engage in healthy forms of communication with teachers and peers. Few opportunities to express their needs for support in constructive ways.	Students do not feel like they have a voice in school, or an opportunity for constructive dialogue and communication with their teachers and peers.	Joanna provides communication logs as an opportunity for students to share their feelings and needs for support directly with her. These communication logs can take different forms depending on student needs. Students can use visuals to communicate their goals, as seen in Figures 5.1 and 5.2.	Students keep active journals with their teacher to provide a dialogue and share any issues or areas of need directly. Joanna provides the option for students to communicate through their writing and visually through drawings or graphic designs via their Chromebooks.

made them feel are the consequences of punitive approaches rather than recognizing their humanity.

Kaba (2021) argues that true abolition and transformation of schools must include a complete divestment from any disciplinary approaches that are not fully restorative, humanizing, and enacted with community. This includes the eradication of systems that serve to punish and dehumanize, such as prisons and, in the case of schools, expulsions, suspensions, and other forms of segregation. As Joanna's story indicates, punitive forms of punishment for her male minority students with disabilities only served to make them feel isolated and devalued in schools. As a teacher who is working toward true transformation of the system of special education and the ways youth of color are being disciplined, Joanna's fight continues to be one for abolition and reform.

In an ideal world, Joanna envisions a space where consequences that prioritize exclusion are eradicated for all students. Instead, she envisions education as abolitionist. Spring (2016) suggests that school abolition would seek to end dehumanizing practices that are often reserved for Black and Brown youth and youth with disabilities. Additionally, abolitionist education would work to dismantle the conditions of white supremacy and ableism that uphold what we currently know as traditional schooling. For example, Joanna notes how ableism is prevalent in the language we use when referring to students (e.g., low functioning, troubled) and the ways her Black and Brown students with disabilities are excluded from their general education classrooms simply for existing. Even without having what are deemed as problematic behaviors, Black and Brown students with disabilities are already seen as incapable of being educated in general education environments with same-aged peers (Annamma et al., 2013).

Because of the role of what Joanna coined as "disability battle fatigue" for special education teachers of color (Kulkarni et al., 2022), special education teachers of color often fight against the injustices of exclusion more generally in addition to exclusionary discipline practices. This double-edged sword makes it even more critical for special education teachers of color like Joanna to understand how ableism and racism co-operate in schools and in her specific role as a special education teacher of predominantly male students of color with disabilities. In dreaming beyond her current circumstances, Joanna envisions an anti-racist, anti-ableist school space where students are included and accepted, where teachers and students work together to co-create expectations around behavior and discipline, and where students of color with disabilities feel like their humanity is recognized.

References

Annamma, S. (2016). Disrupting the carceral state through education journey mapping. *International Journal of Qualitative Studies in Education, 29*(9), 1210–1230.

Annamma, S. A., Connor, D., & Ferri, B. (2013). Dis/ability critical race studies (DisCrit): Theorizing at the intersections of race and dis/ability. *Race Ethnicity and Education, 16*(1), 1–31.

Artiles, A. J., & Jacks, L. L. (n.d.). Beyond the essential other: Engaging disability intersections in teacher education. In *Equity alliance, equity matters: In learning, for life*. Stanford Graduate School of Education. https://equityalliance.stanford.edu/node/203

Carter, P. L., Skiba, R., Arredondo, M. I., & Pollock, M. (2017). You can't fix what you don't look at: Acknowledging race in addressing racial discipline disparities. *Urban Education, 52*(2), 207–235.

Cruz, R. A., Kulkarni, S. S., & Firestone, A. R. (2021). A QuantCrit analysis of context, discipline, special education, and disproportionality. *AERA Open, 7*, 23328584211041354.

Gage, N. A., Whitford, D. K., Katsiyannis, A., Adams, S., & Jasper, A. (2019). National analysis of the disciplinary exclusion of black students with and without disabilities. *Journal of Child and Family Studies, 28*, 1754–1764.

Kaba, M. (2021). *We do this' til we free us: Abolitionist organizing and transforming justice* (Vol. 1). Haymarket Books.

Kulkarni, S., Kim, S. Y., & Holdman, N. (2024). Using virtual learning labs to (re)mediate exclusionary discipline policies for young children of color with disabilities. *Critical Education, 15*, 110–131.

Kulkarni, S. S., Bland, S., & Gaeta, J. M. (2022). From support to action: A critical affinity group of special education teachers of color. *Teacher Education and Special Education, 45*(1), 43–60.

Meiners, E. R., & Winn, M. T. (Eds.). (2012). *Education and incarceration*. Routledge.

Spring, J. (2016). *Deculturalization and the struggle for humanity: A brief history of dominated cultures in the United States*. Routledge.

6

ASHLEY

Unlearning Racism and Ableism Alongside Disabled Students of Color in High School

With Contributions by Ashley Highsmith-Johnson

> *Empathy is not simply a matter of trying to imagine what others are going through, but having the will to muster enough courage to do something about it. In a way, empathy is predicated upon hope.*
> —Cornel West

Ashley, a high school teacher of students with extensive support needs in the Central Valley of California, often talks infectiously about how meaningful racial representation has been for her as a Black, female special education teacher and when she was a Black, school-aged girl. When she was in my (Saili's) credential and master's program courses at San José State, Ashley would light up when she recalled seeing storybooks with Black characters and Black hair for the first time or when she had her first Black teacher. It was the same way she became enthusiastic when she read a set of excerpts from David Connor's book *Urban Narratives*, which chronicled the journeys of high school students of color with learning disabilities. Representation mattered then and continues to matter for Ashley.

Although not a Black, female special education teacher, I empathized with that level of excitement at the first time seeing someone who looks like you in a field dominated by white women. In one such instance, I remember meeting Subini Annamma, one of the authors of DisCrit theory (Annamma et al., 2013), in a bathroom at a Council for Exceptional Children Conference while I was a doctoral student. The excitement of feeling like I wasn't the only South Asian female doing this work was unparalleled. It can be isolating . . . being the only one. For Ashley, part of her work of being a

DOI: 10.4324/9781003653783-7

special education teacher of color was to help her students see that they weren't alone. The other part was to help her students realize that there were systems at play: ableism and racism specifically that kept her students from meaningful participation in schools and their community, from being seen as whole, and from reaching their full potential. Ashley additionally set out to encourage her students to become agents of change in their local communities by recognizing some of these specific injustices.

In a field where teacher candidates are mostly white, especially in special education, and both preparation programs and classroom spaces rarely interrogate oppression, white comfort has given way to deficit framing of students, families, and communities from nondominant backgrounds (Gist, 2017). As was shared in the introduction to this book, research on special education teachers of color did not really exist until about 2018. This indicates just how pervasively white the special education workforce is and how little attention has been paid to authentic representation of teachers of color.

In this chapter, we (Ashley and Saili) share Ashley's background and experiences leading up to her current work as a special education teacher of color supporting students of color with extensive support needs in a high school community transition program. Ashley shares some of the ways that she tries to cultivate representation for her students of color with disabilities and follows with specific strategies and supports she uses to actively resist structures of racism and ableism and help her students combat these systems.

Background and History

Strangely enough, teaching wasn't the first career I (Ashley) thought about for myself. For a long time, I really had no idea what I wanted to do, but I knew that helping my community was important to me. Growing up, there were two teachers I had who truly believed in me and shaped who I was as a student. The first teacher was Mrs. Craft, my first-grade teacher. She pushed me in a gentle and loving way that made me believe in myself. The second teacher was Mr. Orsi, my high school government teacher, who gave us creative freedom and challenged us to want to truly understand history through a critical lens and how our country worked to systematically marginalize certain groups of people. He did this through innovative and engaging assignments. Best of all, he listened to us and tried to make learning as easy and fun as possible. As one of the only teachers of color I had in school, Mr. Orsi's approach to education helped steer me in the direction of wanting to help students through the same lens of kindness and critique.

When I was 18, I started tutoring and became a classroom aide. In this space, I fell in love with supporting students with disabilities and their goals. In particular, there was one student at the middle school whom I worked with one-on-one. His name was Curtis. I could talk about Curtis for days. He heavily contributed to my desire to work in the field of education. To be completely honest, when I got the job working as an aide, I had no idea what it meant to support a student with a disability; all I knew was that I was to be an aide for a student, Curtis, who had an autism diagnosis. Working alongside Curtis changed my life. When he went to high school, and I finished my bachelor's degree, I knew that I wanted to continue working in special education. I learned as much from him as he had learned from me.

Challenges With Special Education

My role as an aide in a special education middle school classroom was at a school site in my local community. Teaching in the area where I lived, however, had its own challenges. I've had challenges trying to figure out who I am and what I represent. Specifically, I think about what it means to be a Black special education teacher when most teachers around me, and a lot of the leadership, are white. I think about how this plays into how I am perceived by my peers and administrators.

I've also had challenges with my lack of knowledge. Being an intern teacher when I didn't have that much of a special education background yet was something I have had to resonate with. My first year of lead teaching was by far one of the toughest teaching years I have ever had. I was basically learning on the job and trying to stay afloat. I was teaching a classroom of 14 boys, grades 1–6, with each student having a different disability. It was *tough*. I remember going home every other night crying. I struggled with not being fully trained on how to write IEPs, how to use the appropriate classroom management tools, and being unaware of how to balance the life of being both a teacher candidate (student) and lead teacher. After that first year, I also quickly realized that elementary school was not for me.

After teaching students with disabilities at the elementary level, I went into a secondary program in the Bay Area and absolutely loved it! I felt as though I was able to grow, learn, and observe from teachers/mentors/ professors who either looked like me or had the same passion for education as me. I realized that high school fulfilled something in me that I wasn't getting from elementary school-aged students. I wanted to work with young adults and really support their transition from high school to the outside world. It felt (and continues to feel) like a meaningful profession, helping

96 Racism and Ableism in the Classroom and Teacher Education

students generate their identities as people in the world. Although I loved this new position and working/living in a part of the Bay Area where I had teachers and staff who looked like me, I had family obligations that drew me back to the Central Valley.

Eventually, I moved to the Central Valley, and new challenges arose. I quickly learned how the Central Valley is not as progressive and diverse as the Bay Area, despite having a large majority of students with disabilities from the Latinx community. I worked in a district where I saw mistreatment of minority students, and whenever I tried to speak up about it, I would get penalized. For example, I once tried to defend a student who was being placed in a segregated environment for his challenging behavior, and because of my vocality, I was later prevented from receiving some resources for my classroom. The whole experience was just so defeating that I kept having internal struggles about whether I should continue teaching or belong as a special education teacher in this context. It took a lot of soul-searching and resilience to continue working as a teacher after those negative experiences.

Representation

Honestly, I wish I saw more of me in the teaching field. I think about that a lot. As I shared before, I only had one other teacher of color between elementary school and high school. One Black teacher. Even in college, I had only one Black teacher. It makes me think that if I could share one thing with other special education teachers of color, it would be to persist. At the very least, we need to see more of us in the field. We need little Black girls and boys to know that they can become teachers and how critical it is to our representation both in the field and in the practices we use to support Black and Brown babies in schools. First and foremost, our students need to be able to relate to us racially and culturally.

One of my favorite memories when I taught at the elementary school occurred when I was wearing my natural hair in a curly ponytail. A little girl came up to me in the hallway and gave me her special clothes pin for the day. The clothes pin showed that she had a great day at school and she was permitted to keep it or give it to someone she was thankful for. She came up to me and gave me a clothes pin. She smiled and said, "I'm grateful for you because we have the same hair Miss. H!" She hugged me and ran off. I looked at my staff picture and noticed I was the only Black woman at that school, a school with a high percentage of Black students. I was someone who walked through the halls, and all of the little Black girls recognized me and would smile and wave.

Overall, yes, there are so many challenges with special education. The way my students of color are treated, the way I am treated, how my knowledge is constantly questioned, and the way I have the weight of so many Black babies and Black special educators on my back. It can be overwhelming at times. As a Black woman and a teacher in special education, I have had to consistently prove myself across the board. But I keep pushing. Because of those challenges and growing lessons, I can look at the students who smile at me and know that it is all worth it.

Unlearning Internalized Racism and Ableism

When other teachers and administrators would question my knowledge of my students and how to best support them, it sometimes made me question whether I was indeed doing things the right way. I started to have this inferiority complex. For a while, I thought I wasn't good enough, and although I was taking courses to become credentialed and earning strong grades in all of my courses, it still felt like I wasn't good enough. Earning my master's degree and having the support of my professors in the master's and credential program was one of the ways I began to recognize my own potential. When some of my professors embraced my knowledge and experience as a *Black* special education teacher and actually valued these things, it showed me that I didn't have to question myself anymore. The feedback I would receive from my students, their families, and my professors enabled me to be a more confident and compassionate educator.

Instead of focusing my attention on the things I couldn't do, I began to lean into the ways I could make a difference with my students with disabilities. For example, my social nature allowed me to build strong relationships with the families of my students, their service providers, and local businesses. For example, when I started working with young adults, having connections with local businesses allowed them to get vocational job training opportunities. My newly formed confidence also allowed me to become a more vocal advocate for my students when other teachers or administrators tended to segregate or underestimate their abilities. This shift also led me to consider new ways of thinking about racism and ableism as they show up in schools, both for me as a teacher and my students as learners.

Unlearning Racism and Ableism With High School Students

I (Saili) met Ashley as part of her master's program in special education at San José State University. Part of Ashley's unlearning of racism and ableism came through her teacher education program and opportunities to grapple with what it meant to be a Black special education teacher in a mostly white field and a mostly white school district. In particular, she also shared how the Black community still needed to recognize how it perpetuates ableism despite being impacted by it. Broderick and Leonardo (2015) describe how smartness and goodness are used to position students of color from a young age. In my 2021 article (Kulkarni, 2021), I draw from this framework to describe how special education teachers of color are positioned as less smart and good in teacher education programs and their classrooms and how this builds upon the trajectory of their lives as students of color. In Ashley's case, her journey as a special education teacher of color, including her teacher education program and prior experiences working with students with disabilities, illustrates a pattern of being actively challenged for resisting dominant ideologies of race and ability.

Entangled within the complexities of how she grapples with her community and their perpetuation of ableism is the backdrop of her experiences working with disabled young adults of color as one of the few Black special education teachers in her district. Ashley's current role supports young adults with extensive support needs in community-based instructional settings. In that role, she described how resisting ableist and racist narratives of her role and her students required her to be a *vocal advocate for disabled youth of color in the community*. She needed to support her students in learning to see themselves as leaders and self-advocates after they exited special education services at the age of 22.

Furthermore, Ashley worked closely with her students and their families to build relationships with local organizations and job sites to provide her students with experiences that matched their individual interests and goals. For example, she partnered with local coffee shops in the Central Valley to help her students obtain employment. Beyond this work for vocational experience, however, Ashley advocated for the coffee shops to provide her students with the necessary accommodations and resources for supported employment. She created direct changes in the environment to support her students' disabilities.

Additionally, Ashley built relationships with job sites that actively employed a variety of individuals across disability and race. She shared that she wanted to help her students to feel like they weren't *the only*. Therefore, Ashley created *representative supported employment opportunities* for her students of color with disabilities. For example, in Figure 6.1, we can see a couple of the other employment venues that Ashley utilized for her students. These include the relationships she built with the local zoo, Goodwill, and Poverello House, a homeless shelter in the Fresno area. These venues emphasize what Ashley envisions for her students, which is

Thursday November 21st, 2024

Work
- Poverello House
- The Zoo
- Goodwill

Mrs. Sanchez lesson

FIGURE 6.1 Work Opportunities for Ashley's Students

to have employment opportunities that are varied and also incorporate a diverse group of employees.

Simi Linton (1998) shared how people with disabilities are all connected, not because they have impairments or deficits, but because they have experienced the social and political circumstances that come from ableism. Part of Ashley's role, therefore, was to also help her students with extensive support needs to build pride in their identities and disabilities. To do this, Ashley had to begin by *helping her students understand their disabilities and begin to counter ableism and internalized ableism.* Unlearning ableism was a big part of Ashley's own transition as a special education teacher and a teacher of color.

In order to counter ableism and her students' internalized ableism, Ashley began by providing her students with opportunities to recognize where stigma and inequities occur within school and then moved to the community level. In the classroom, she worked with her students to identify the places where ableism might exist. For example, her students had open discussions about physical space and why they were segregated from the rest of the school community. They had discussions about why the only interaction with the general high school population was when someone would come to "volunteer" or "help" in the classroom. After exposing these localized inequities, Ashley and her students moved toward a broader understanding of ableism. They identified where in the community access was and wasn't present. For example, students would be on a community

100 Racism and Ableism in the Classroom and Teacher Education

walk and identify where someone in the classroom who used a wheelchair wouldn't be able to glide across a sidewalk due to a lack of curb cut. Students also looked at how individuals in the community interacted with them, whether the reaction was pity, an overeagerness to help do things *for* the students, or if students were valued as individuals. Ashley chose regular outings and spaces to help students recognize these instances of ableism in the community.

Conclusion

Baglieri and Lalvani (2019) shared that "people deemed disabled are treated and experience their lives based on gender, race, and social class" (p. 50). Ashley's work as a high school special education teacher of color working with young adults of color with disabilities centered the importance of representation. As someone who had her own share of experiences

TABLE 6.1 Summary of Connection and Community-Engaged Practices

Practice	Description	Reframing	Example
Students of color with disabilities in vocational training are often set up with jobs where they are taught to adapt to the conditions of the work environment.	Roberts and Leko (2013) describe how students with intellectual disabilities often lack the "adaptive skills" focused on in the work environment. The framing of vocational training is often from the perspective of employer needs versus generating an accessible environment.	While providing support and adaptive skill development are important, Ashley simultaneously focused on teaching the place of employment how to best support her students of color with extensive support needs.	Connections with local coffee shops, Goodwill, and homeless shelters as partners for employment for her students of color with disabilities. Ashley worked with the employers to provide necessary support and accommodations to her students. For example, for one of her students, the employer was provided with a strategy to constantly provide positive reinforcement for completing job-related tasks such as taking inventory, emptying the cash register, and greeting customers.

(Continued)

Ashley **101**

TABLE 6.1 (Continued)

Practice	Description	Reframing	Example
Students of color with disabilities in vocational training programs are often asked to find jobs based on general level of interest versus an environment based on diversity, equity, and inclusion.	Students of color with disabilities are often provided with jobs that match a surface level of general interest rather than a specific interest. Furthermore, there are times when they are *the only* person of color or disabled employee.	Ashley worked with local businesses that had representation in terms of racial, linguistic, and ability differences. The coffee shops and other places where her students received job training prioritized diversity, equity, and inclusion.	Ashley used her strong voice and advocacy skills to seek out specific businesses that would prioritize diversity, equity and inclusion (DEI). For example, she looked for businesses such as Goodwill and the zoo (seen in Figure 6.1) that had clearly displayed DEI statements and worked with businesses that valued diverse representation among their staff.
Students of color with disabilities are often provided community inclusion opportunities that ask that they adapt to an inaccessible and ableist environment.	Often community inclusion programs are focused on how individuals with disabilities can adapt to an inaccessible and ableist environment.	Ashley strived to help her students (a) learn about their own disabilities and (b) recognize how ableism operates in the community.	Using specific assignments related to ableism, Ashley helped her students identify where there were inaccessible spaces in the community. For example, students had to identify sidewalks where curb cuts were omitted or recognize bus drivers whose comments toward them were genuine vs. patronizing (e.g., "bless you, son"). These little things eventually helped her students of color with disabilities to see themselves and their disability from the viewpoint of pride vs. impairment.

as *the only*. Ashley worked hard to establish opportunities so that her students wouldn't feel that way in their place of employment and their communities. In order to actively unlearn ableism, in particular, Ashley shifted the onus of responsibility in supported employment opportunities from her students of color with disabilities to the employers and places of business. Her work building relationships with local companies to create accessible environments for her students, in particular, was critical to generating disability-friendly spaces. Additionally, Ashley made it so that these environments were also sensitive to racial, linguistic, and ability representation. While someone has to be the first, Ashley ensured that her students were in the position to build allyship and community with others.

Like Alice Wong (2020), who shared that she wanted to see herself in the books on bookshelves, Ashley wanted to be able to have her students see themselves in their fellow employees. I (Ashley) want my students to be able to look around their workplace and see themselves in other employees there. Although I still don't see that many teachers like me where I work, I am hoping that things will be different for them in their careers. My students are the reason I persist despite all of the issues I have with being one of the few Black special education teachers in my district. As I mentioned before, I am hoping that more special education teachers of color, and especially Black special education teachers, will persist because we need to have students relate to us and see themselves in us. I am hoping that someday things will be different for both my students and teachers in the workplace.

References

Annamma, S. A., Connor, D., & Ferri, B. (2013). Dis/ability critical race studies (DisCrit): Theorizing at the intersections of race and dis/ability. *Race Ethnicity and Education, 16*(1), 1–31.

Baglieri, S., & Lalvani, P. (2019). *Undoing ableism: Teaching about disability in K-12 classrooms*. Routledge.

Broderick, A. A., & Leonardo, Z. (2015). What a good boy. In *DisCrit-disability studies and critical race theory in education* (pp. 55–67). Teachers College Press.

Connor, D. J. (2008). *Urban narratives: Portraits in progress, life at the intersections of learning disability, race, & social class* (Vol. 5). Peter Lang.

Gist, C. D. (2017). Culturally responsive pedagogy for teachers of color. *The New Educator, 13*(3), 288–303.

Kulkarni, S. S. (2021). Special education teachers of color and their beliefs about dis/ability and race: Counter-stories of smartness and goodness. *Curriculum Inquiry, 51*(5), 496–521.

Linton, S. (1998). *Claiming disability: Knowledge and identity*. New York University Press.

Roberts, C. A., & Leko, M. M. (2013). Integrating functional and academic goals into literacy instruction for adolescents with significant cognitive disabilities through shared story reading. *Research and Practice for Persons with Severe Disabilities, 38*(3), 157–172.

Wong, A. (Ed.). (2020). *Disability visibility: First-person stories from the twenty-first century*. Vintage.

7

GRAPPLING WITH RACISM AND ABLEISM IN SPECIAL EDUCATION

Special Education Teachers of Color and Resistance

Barclay (2021) shared how the pervasive rhetoric around slavery and Black bodies during the antebellum years was one of race, dependency, and infantilization. Blackness was connected to "disability, defectiveness and dependency" while whiteness evoked a sense of "normality, wholeness, vitality and rationality" (p. 1). The history of the enslavement of Black people, cultural assimilation of Indigenous peoples deemed as "re-education," and other examples of oppression are the backbone of the U.S. school system. In the current school system, we can see remnants of this history of suppression and segregation in the education of Black, Indigenous Peoples of Color (BIPOC), and those multiply marginalized across race, ability, and disability. Tefera et al. (2023) coined the term "DefectCraft" to describe how a suburban school district interpreted high disproportionate representation of Black students in special education programs. Specifically, they used DefectCraft to describe how school systems erase or evade intersectional oppressions in their understanding of students' academic and socio-behavioral school outcomes.

Glossing over the dehumanizing and oppressive histories of BIPOC students in schools has continued to be a pervasive practice in both special education and school systems overall (Tefera et al., 2023). It captures what LaVeda, Loriann, Samuel, Joanna, and Ashley all share about their own experiences going through school and what they attempt to resist in their work as special education teachers of color. Tackling the institutional structures of racism and ableism in their classrooms was not something that was deeply addressed in their traditional special education teacher education programs. For these five individuals, their deep commitments to anti-racist,

DOI: 10.4324/9781003653783-8

anti-ableist education for their students led to a search for outside opportunities and professional learning to supplement a traditionally structured teacher education program.

Tensions With Special Education and Teacher Education Curriculum

University-based special education teacher education programs play a critical role in disrupting, shaping, maintaining, or perpetuating how teacher candidates experience ableism (Keefe, 2022) and racism (Kohli & Pizarro, 2022). In early childhood special education teacher education programs, for example, efforts to professionalize licensure have often led to a heavy focus on developmentalism, which largely serves a white, able-bodied population (Love & Hancock, 2022).

Furthermore, across the spectrum of special education teacher education, research has centered the knowledge and experiences of the white women, and pre-service teacher education research has attended heavily to this population (Beneke et al., 2022; Siuty et al., 2024). White women continue to be centered in research on special education teacher preparation and how to support their intersectional racial literacy (Sleeter, 2008; Harry & Klingner, 2014). Siuty et al. (2024) in particular note how teacher preparation programs that are deemed "urban" often must contend with a white saviorism complex that plagues these spaces but miss how ableism is critically examined.

Special education teacher education curriculum, in line with such research, has continued to maintain racist, ableist, and behaviorist traditions at the detriment of students and teachers of color. In line with DefectCraft (Tefera et al., 2023), when probed about why the curriculum decenters intersectional oppression, most leaders cite issues of time and a need to link to rigid state and federal education standards. If there was a strong commitment to decentering whiteness and ableism in these spaces, however, programs should push to incorporate representative and meaningful curriculum that supports candidates' unlearning racism and ableism across entire programs (Kulkarni et al., 2024).

The Case for Disability-Centered Culturally Sustaining Pedagogies (DCCSPs)

The need for curriculum that centers disability and race has been argued in order to eradicate "dysfunctional classroom ecologies" (Annamma & Morrison, 2018a, 2018b), which highlight how multiply marginalized students of color with disabilities are dehumanized in school settings. Annamma and Morrison (2018a) specifically note how a DisCrit classroom ecology includes (1) a DisCrit curriculum that teaches about structural inequities and learns student histories; (2) a DisCrit Pedagogy to highlight students' gifts; and (3) a DisCrit Solidarity in order to create joint efforts to resist hegemonic and oppressive school systems.

My earlier work to dismantle overly racist, behaviorist, and ableist special education teacher education curriculum resulted in reimagining the two courses to integrate more dynamic readings (see Kulkarni, 2021; Table 1). However, in order to truly build off of a DisCrit classroom ecology and the idea that anti-ableist and anti-racist education needs to be explicit in both teacher education and P-12 classrooms, we introduced a conceptual framework and pedagogical application known as Disability-Centered Culturally Sustaining Pedagogies (DCCSPs; Kulkarni et al., 2024).

DCCSPs incorporate five key principles that build off of the existing work of DisCrit (Annamma et al., 2013) and the loving critiques that inform culturally sustaining pedagogies (Alim & Paris, 2017). Primarily, DCCSPs promote (1) asset-framing of multiply marginalized disabled youth of color, (2) understanding of activist and poverty scholars' lived experiences in centering multiply marginalized disabled youth of color, (3) embracing the identities of multiply marginalized disabled peoples, (4) understanding of how multiple and intersecting oppressions advance white supremacy and ableism, and (5) encouraging resistance and activism *with* disabled youth of color (see Figure 7.1).

Actively Building Resistance and Cultivating Joy With Multiply Marginalized Disabled Students of Color

Stewart (2021) in her book *The Politics of Joy: Zora Neale-Hurston and Neo-Abolitionism* shares

> my upbringing is sown with scenes of Black joy. The simply sinful spread of crawfish, corn, and potatoes under the oaks in my grandfather's yard as my extended family ate and ate until the cicadas chimed in with our music late in the evening. Birthday horse rides at the stable of my great-uncle, the (self-proclaimed) first Black cowboy in Ascension Parish. . . . Above all, I had a fierce sense that what I witnessed and participated in could not be reduced to merely a reaction against the racism that brands this region in our national imagination. In fact, I was acutely aware of how much of our everyday lives seemed to not revolve around white folks.

PRINCIPLES OF DISABILITY-CENTERED, CULTURALLY SUSTAINING PEDAGOGIES IN TEACHER EDUCATION

1 ASSET FRAMING MULTIPLY MARGINALIZED DISABLED YOUTH OF COLOR
Prepares and supports teachers in using asset framing of multiply marginalized disabled youth of color and critiques how schools perpetuate hegemonic cultural priactices.
DisCrit Tenet One: Racism & Ableism as Interdependent
CSP Loving Critique One: Cultural and Linguistic Repertoires of Disabled Youth of Color

2 UNDE RSTAINDI NG DISABLED ACTIVISTS & POVERTY SCHOLARS' LIVED EXPERIENCES TO CENTER MULTIPLY MARGINALIZED DISABLED YOUTH OF COLOR
Prepares teachers to reveal the gifts, resistance, solutions, and ordinary lives of disabled activists and poverty scholars, in centering multiply marginalized disabled youth of color in classrooms.
DisCrit Tenet Four: Emphasizes Voices of Multiply Marginalized Groups & Individuals
CSP Loving Critique Two: Fluid Understanding of Culture, How Youth Live identities

3 EMBRACING MULTIPLY MARGINALIZED DISABLED IDENTITIES
Prepares teachers to uphold the knowledge and expertise of disabled activists of colar and poverty scholars as models for youth to 'live" their identitleis through joyful recognition and create their own culture.
DisCrit Tenet Five: How Race & Disability Used Legally & Historically to Deny Rights
CSP Loving Critique Two: Fluid Understanding of Culture, How Youth Live identities

4 RECOGNIZING MULTIPLE AND INTERSECTING OPPRESSIONS AS ADVANCING WHITE SUPREMACY AND ABLEISM
Implores teachers in recognizing how racism and ableism are linked and wihy disability services and supports privilege white people. Recognizes that multiply marginalized people con also consciously and/or unconsciously perpetucite harm.
Discrit Tenet Six: Whiteness & Ability as Property
CSP Loving Critique 3: Look Inward: How Oppressed Communities Can Reproduce Inequity

5 ENCOURAGING RESISTANCE AND ACTIVISM WITH! MULTIPLY MARGINALIZED DISABLED YOUTH OF COLOR
Encourages teachers to honor students epistemologies, ontological orientations, and resistance(s) of hegemonic notions of knowledge. Teachers respond to youth resistance through particular ideological and pedagogical shifts engaging in expansive forms of resistance and activism.
DisCrit Tenet Seven: Resistance S Activism
CSP Loving Critique One: Cultural and Linguistic Repertoires of Disabled Youth of Color

FIGURE 7.1   Principles of DCCSP

Each of the special education teachers of color who shared their stories in this book sought to move away from special education practices steeped in whiteness and ableism toward something more meaningful and joyful for their students and themselves. In thinking specifically about the experiences and practices shared by LaVeda, Loriann, Samuel, Joanna, and Ashley, each special education teacher of color envisioned ways to actively resist the hegemonic, oppressive structures of racism and ableism that perpetuated their experiences as students, teacher candidates, and classroom teachers. Many of these teachers worked closely with our collective to unlearn racism and ableism in the classroom through intentional professional development sessions that were led by poverty scholars and community activists with disabilities (see Brown et al., 2023).

As current and former special education teachers, each teacher noted some of the systemic barriers to actively resisting and dismantling oppressive systems across their classrooms and contexts. For some, the forces of ableism and racism in classrooms were too much weight, and they noted how fighting systems of oppression with the limited power of a teacher proved to be too challenging. Specifically for Samuel and Loriann, much of their additional efforts to advocate for their multiply marginalized disabled students of color were not met with support from their leadership. In Loriann's case, she decided to become a school leader in hopes of using this power to advocate for students more broadly. In Samuel's case, he found that anti-ableist practices can be generated anywhere, even if not in a traditional classroom space.

Across each of their stories, however, each special education teacher of color moved away from a status quo approach to educating students with disabilities toward the fifth principle of DCCSPs. Each teacher, in other words, actively built education *with* rather than *for* multiply marginalized disabled students of color.

For example, Ashley's position as a community-based high school special education teacher was focused on providing young adults with the skills to hold down a vocation. Rather than placing students based on their skills, however, Ashley actively looked for ways to help her students feel seen and valued in their job placements. She built connections with local businesses, garnered direct input from students, and helped support their transition based on their unique desires and wishes. Additionally, she ensured that students saw themselves as one of many employees of color in a welcoming and inclusive work environment.

For Samuel, an experience in desegregating education through the National Endowment for the Humanities helped shape an identity as a Black, male special education teacher. Through the lesson plan on Brown vs. Board of Education and some of the disadvantages of implementing the

108 Racism and Ableism in the Classroom and Teacher Education

integration of Black students in white schools, Samuel was able to draw parallels to the current education system for students of color with disabilities. Samuel was able to draw upon history to help students understand the concepts of belonging and identity and to reflect on their own experiences with schooling. These activities helped students to understand the broader structures of ableism and racism that can inform identity development and imposter syndrome: how Black and Brown students with disabilities are made to feel inferior to their white, able-bodied peers in schools.

For Joanna, sense of belongingness was also what she hoped to cultivate for her population of male minority students with disabilities in a middle school setting. Learning about her students' experiences as cast out from the school, both physically through suspensions and expulsions and socially deemed as kids who were not "smart or good" created an inferiority complex for them that she had to work to undo through reflective exercises and journey mapping. Joanna's approach was not about changing students' behavior to meet a system of exclusion and dehumanization, but rather about helping the administration and staff recognize her male minority students with disabilities and their humanity.

Loriann too wanted to move away from a system of dehumanization so often used with young children of color with disabilities. In her work as an elementary special education teacher, Loriann incorporated principles of restorative justice into her practice. These practices were a lens through which she approached not only her teaching but also her collaboration with adults. Loriann worked to decenter whiteness and ability as property in her classroom (Kulkarni & Chong, 2021) and approached her students as active contributors to classroom and school culture.

Similarly, for LaVeda, allowing her students to celebrate their youth through movement, dance, and song rather than exercising excessive control over their bodies led to the enactment of joy and a classroom culture of love and acceptance. Students in LaVeda's classroom felt welcome, represented, and excited about being in a nurturing learning space. LaVeda's commitment to her community and move toward treating her young students as valuable contributors of knowledge illustrates how she resists dominant narratives about Black and Brown disabled bodies, the capabilities of young children, and the importance of a classroom that cultivates joy.

Moving Forward: Resistance Not Resilience

This book incorporated the intentional progression of cases of special education teachers of color from LaVeda, who taught as an early childhood special education, to Loriann, who taught elementary school students with

Grappling With Racism and Ableism in Special Education **109**

disabilities as a resource specialist, to Samuel and Joanna, who both taught middle school students with disabilities, and finally, Ashley, who worked with high school and transition-aged students with disabilities. Each of these special education teachers of color shared narratives from their experiences in a mix of segregated and inclusive settings and across the state of California. While their stories across teacher education and practices with multiply marginalized disabled students of color are unique to their own experiences, there are shared understandings that resonate across each case narrative and similarly for special education teachers of color working broadly across the United States. The challenges and tools each of these teachers shared have strong implications for research across teacher education and practice in the field of special education and recommendations for policy and practice level shifts. I provide three key areas of consideration below that address these critical shifts.

Deinstitutionalize Special Education

More than 50 years ago in the United States, individuals with disabilities saw a shift in how they were perceived and educated. Specifically, individuals with disabilities who were often placed in segregated institutions became part of a deinstitutionalization movement that enabled public educational access (Jones & Gallus, 2016). Intentionally and subversively, however, the multiple and intersecting oppressions of racism and ableism created a new type of institutionalization for students of color with disabilities. Although a part of public school instruction, students of color with disabilities continue to receive education in segregated classrooms with watered-down curricula and limited post-secondary outcomes.

Connor et al.'s (2024) open letter to the field of special education notes how despite over three decades of research on inclusive education, there are some who remain skeptical about the benefits of having students with or without disabilities in the same classroom space. The continued segregation of students across disability status and race was perceived and felt deeply by each of the special education teachers chronicled in this book. As practitioners broadly situated across the state of California, across grade level and categorical assignment, it is telling that none of the five teachers worked in a full inclusion classroom program. For the teachers who provided intervention and pull-out services as resource specialists, their students continued to experience segregation from grade-level peers for core academic subjects such as math and reading. As Joanna remarked, for example, students were being denied access to critical social learning opportunities such as field trips and extracurricular activities based on their perceived behavior.

110 Racism and Ableism in the Classroom and Teacher Education

Therefore, it is necessary, given the ongoing challenges to inclusive education in California and across the United States, to *deinstitutionalize* special education. By this I mean that we need to move toward the original intent of the principle of Least Restrictive Environment (LRE), which was intended to keep all students in general education and only sparingly (and in the most extreme circumstances) segregate or separate students with disabilities. In practice, however, special education continues to be equated with a specialized and separate placement for students with disabilities. As Connor et al. (2024) noted, there has been a "historic tendency to place students with disabilities in segregated settings" (p. 1). A true deinstitutionalization of special education would move the field back toward the democratic ideal of inclusive education. As Connor et al. (2024) explain, authentic forms of inclusive education benefit multiply marginalized disabled students of color and create racially, socially, and economically diverse classroom spaces where students can learn about and celebrate difference.

Deinstitutionalization of special education is also necessary in order to prevent what Ben-Moshe (2020) describes as state-sanctioned institutionalization. Multiply marginalized disabled students of color who are educated in segregated settings are more likely to become part of a school-to-prison nexus (Meiners & Winn, 2012) and experience other poor post-school outcomes such as unemployment or homelessness. The special education teachers of color featured in this book worked/work tirelessly to prevent their multiply marginalized disabled students of color from experiencing injustice; however, many were entrenched in a system that deemed their efforts and their students as disposable. A true deinstitutionalization of special education that focuses on including all students in general education settings in authentic and meaningful ways capitalizes on the expertise and dedication of special education teachers of color actively engaging in resistance.

Focus on Resistance Not Resilience

Each of the special education teachers of color featured in this book was actively involved in resistance to systemic structures of injustice that are housed within their schools and the broader field of special education. Like the fifth principle of DCCSPs, each special education teacher of color was/ is engaged in resistance and activism through critical practices that centered their multiply marginalized disabled students of color. It is important, however, to distinguish this feature of their determination and resolve from *resilience*. Resilience (and other qualifiers such as grit) suggests that the responsibility for combatting oppressive racist and ableist school systems should fall on special education teachers of color. Instead, we must focus on how these special education teachers of color actively resist these systems of oppression. For some of them, this meant leaving racist/ableist field of special education. It is telling that many of the teachers have moved in search of supportive leadership and a school culture that centers justice. For Loriann and Samuel, it meant exiting special education in search of other ways to address ableism and racism. For LaVeda, Joanna, and Ashley, it meant shifting school sites and/or districts.

This book relied on the wisdom, critical expertise, and resistance of five special education teachers of color across grade level and context in the state of California. The decision to incorporate a broad range of teachers of color illustrates the complexities of special education as a field and a strong need to deinstitutionalize special education in the interest of multiply marginalized disabled youth of color. At the same time, this book also focuses on joy that special education teachers of color carved out within the oppressive spaces of special education. Like Stewart's (2021) book on Zora Neale Hurston and Black joy, disability in education is often experienced as a space of sorrow and deficit. In each of these five teachers' stories, we experience the complexities of resistance and the critical practices that create moments of celebration and joy for their multiply marginalized disabled students of color.

As Zora Neale Hurston (1928) shared in *How It Feels to Be Colored Me*

> I am not tragically colored. There is no great sorrow dammed up in my soul, nor lurking behind my eyes. I do not mind at all. I do not belong to the sobbing school of Negrohood who hold that nature somehow has given them a lowdown dirty deal and whose feelings are all but about it. Even in the helter-skelter skirmish that is my life, I have seen that the world is to the strong regardless of a little pigmentation more or less. No, I do not weep at the world—I am too busy sharpening my oyster knife.

So too are the special education teachers of color "sharpening their oyster knives" in this book moving beyond the tragic and oversimplified versions of a special education teacher as "patient" or "overburdened" by the work with multiply marginalized disabled students of color. Instead, each chooses to focus on addressing racism and ableism within teacher education, their classrooms, and society at large.

References

Alim, H. S., & Paris, D. (2017). What is culturally sustaining pedagogy and why does it matter. *Culturally Sustaining Pedagogies: Teaching and Learning for Justice in a Changing World*, 1(24), 85–101.

112 Racism and Ableism in the Classroom and Teacher Education

Annamma, S., & Morrison, D. (2018a). DisCrit classroom ecology: Using praxis to dismantle dysfunctional education ecologies. *Teaching and Teacher Education, 73*, 70–80.

Annamma, S., & Morrison, D. (2018b). Identifying dysfunctional education ecologies: A DisCrit analysis of bias in the classroom. *Equity & Excellence in Education, 51*(2), 114–131.

Annamma, S. A., Connor, D., & Ferri, B. (2013). Dis/ability critical race studies (DisCrit): Theorizing at the intersections of race and dis/ability. *Race Ethnicity and Education, 16*(1), 1–31.

Barclay, J. L. (2021). *The mark of slavery: Disability, race, and gender in antebellum America.* University of Illinois Press.

Beneke, M. R., Siuty, M. B., & Handy, T. (2022). Emotional geographies of exclusion: Whiteness and ability in teacher education research. *Teachers College Record, 124*(7), 105–130.

Ben-Moshe, L. (2020). *Decarcerating disability: Deinstitutionalization and prison abolition.* University of Minnesota Press.

Brown, L. X., Dickens, B., Gray-Garcia, T. L., Kulkarni, S. S., McLeod, L., Miller, A. L., Nusbaum, E. A., & Pearson, H. (2023). (Re)centering the knowledge of disabled activists, poverty scholars, and community scholars of color to transform education. *Disability Studies Quarterly, 43*(1). https://dsq-sds.org/index.php/dsq/article/view/9693/8022

Connor, D. J., Danforth, S., & Gallagher, D. (2024). An open letter to the field: Contemplating special education's collaborative role in developing inclusive education. *Exceptional Children.* https://doi.org/10.1177/00144029241303051

Harry, B., & Klingner, J. (2014). *Why are so many minority students in special education?: Understanding race and disability in schools.* Teachers College Press.

Hurston, Z. N. (1928). *How it feels to be colored me.* Open Road Media.

Jones, J. L., & Gallus, K. L. (2016). Understanding deinstitutionalization: What families value and desire in the transition to community living. *Research and Practice for Persons with Severe Disabilities, 41*(2), 116–131.

Keefe, E. S. (2022). From detractive to democratic: The duty of teacher education to disrupt structural ableism and reimagine disability. *Teachers College Record, 124*(3), 115–147.

Kohli, R., & Pizarro, M. (2022). The layered toll of racism in teacher education on teacher educators of color. *AERA Open, 8*, 23328584221078538.

Kulkarni, S. S. (2021). Special education teachers of color and their beliefs about dis/ability and race: Counter-stories of smartness and goodness. *Curriculum Inquiry, 51*(5), 496–521.

Kulkarni, S. S., & Chong, M. M. (2021). Teachers of color implementing restorative justice practices in elementary classrooms: A DisCrit analysis. *Equity & Excellence in Education, 54*(4), 378–392.

Kulkarni, S. S., Miller, A. L., Nusbaum, E. A., Pearson, H., & Brown, L. X. (2024). Toward disability-centered, culturally sustaining pedagogies in teacher education. *Critical Studies in Education, 65*(2), 107–127.

Love, H. R., & Hancock, C. L. (2022). Tensions as opportunities for transformation: Applying DisCrit resistance to early childhood teacher education programs. *Contemporary Issues in Early Childhood, 23*(4), 483–499.

Meiners, E. R., & Winn, M. T. (Eds.). (2012). *Education and incarceration.* Routledge.

Siuty, M. B., Beneke, M. R., & Handy, T. (2024). Conceptualizing white-ability saviorism: A necessary reckoning with ableism in urban teacher education. *Review of Educational Research, 95*, 505–535.

Sleeter, C. E. (2008). Preparing white teachers for diverse students. In *Handbook of research on teacher education* (pp. 559–582). Routledge.

Stewart, L. (2021). *The politics of Black joy: Zora Neale Hurston and neo-abolitionism*. Northwestern University Press.

Tefera, A. A., Artiles, A. J., Kramarczuk Voulgarides, C., Aylward, A., & Alvarado, S. (2023). The aftermath of disproportionality citations: Situating disability-race intersections in historical, spatial, and sociocultural contexts. *American Educational Research Journal, 60*(2), 367–404.

APPENDIX A

Table A.1 Curriculum Mapping Teacher
Education Resources on Race and Disability

DCCSP Principle	Sample Engagement Materials	Suggested Course Assignments and Activities
Principle 1: Asset-Framing of Multiply Marginalized Disabled Youth of Color	Connor, D. J. (2008). *Urban narratives: Portraits in progress, life at the intersections of learning disability, race, & social class* (Vol. 5). Peter Lang. Lester, J. N., & Nusbaum, E. A. (2021). *Centering diverse bodyminds in critical qualitative inquiry*. Routledge. Waitoller, F. R., & Thorius, K. K. (Eds.). (2022). *Sustaining disabled youth: Centering disability in asset pedagogies*. Teachers College Press. Wong, A. (2020). *Disability visibility: First-person stories from the twenty-first century*. Vintage Books.	• Short reflections at the end of each class session • Delving deeper into a particular story or perspective through audio, visual, or written project • Using narrative to generate student/family interview questions • Using narrative to co-generate IEP goals with students
Principle 2: Understanding Disabled Activists and Poverty Scholars' Lived Experiences Centering Multiply Marginalized Disabled Youth of Color	Harriet Tubman Collective[1] Krip-Hop Nation (Moore L., 2007)[2] Brown, L. X., Dickens, B., Gray-Garcia, T. L., Kulkarni, S. S., McLeod, L., Miller, A. L., & Pearson, H. (2023). (Re)centering the knowledge of disabled activists, poverty scholars, and community scholars of color to transform education. *Disability Studies Quarterly*, 43(1). McLeod, L. H. (2008). *Declaration of a body of love poetry*. Atahualpa Press.	• Written, audio, or visual in-class reflections • Research for additional materials by community and poverty scholars • Designed lesson plans or units incorporating community and poverty scholar perspectives • Designed lesson plans or units centering disability and poverty in core content (i.e., math, science, reading; see Kulkarni et al., 2023, for examples).

(*Continued*)

DCCSP Principle	Sample Engagement Materials	Suggested Course Assignments and Activities
Principle 3: *Embracing Multiply Marginalized Disabled Identities*	Annamma, S. (2018). *The pedagogy of pathologization: Dis/abled girls of color in the school.* Connor, D., & Ferri, B. A. (2021). *How teaching shapes our thinking about dis/abilities: Stories from the field.* Peter Lang Publishing, Inc. Li, L., Donato-Sapp, H. L., Erevelles, N., Torres, L. E., & Waitoller, F. (2021). A kitchen-table talk against ableism: Disability justice for collective liberation. *Equity & Excellence in Education*, 54(4), 361–374. Hernandez-Saca, D. I. (2020). My learning dis/ability and disability studies in education activism. *Peace Review*, 31(4), 487–496.	• Reflections on authentic representation of disability in media • Reflections on disability representation among teachers/teacher education • Discussions around disabled youth representation and voice/activism • Generating interview or survey for classroom students based on readings and reflections
Principle 4: *Recognizing Multiple and Intersecting Oppressions as Advancing White Supremacy and Ableism*	Baglieri, S., & Lalvani, P. (2019). *Undoing ableism: Teaching about disability in K-12 classrooms.* Routledge. Cioè-Peña, M. (2021). *(M)othering labeled children: Bilingualism and disability in the lives of Latinx mothers* (Vol. 131). Multilingual Matters. Phuong, J., Padía, L., & Beneke, M. R. (2024). Struggling toward abolition and dreaming beyond ableism in teacher education. *Theory Into Practice*, 63(4), 340–352. Siuty, M. B., Beneke, M. R., & Handy, T. (2024). Conceptualizing white-ability saviorism: A necessary reckoning with ableism in urban teacher education. *Review of Educational Research*, 00346543241241336.	• Equity audit of school site, district using Office of Civil Rights and Department of Education data • Generation of a family-teacher relationship-building communication plan • Identifying ableism in everyday interactions • Lesson plans or units directed at teaching about intersectional ableism

(Continued)

DCCSP Principle	Sample Engagement Materials	Suggested Course Assignments and Activities
Tenet 5: Encouraging Resistance and Activism with Multiply Marginalized Disabled Youth of Color	Alim, H. S., & Paris, D. (2017). What is culturally sustaining pedagogy and why does it matter. *Culturally Sustaining Pedagogies: Teaching and Learning for Justice in a Changing World*, 1(24), 85–101. Annamma, S. A., Connor, D., & Ferri, B. (2013). Dis/ability critical race studies (DisCrit): Theorizing at the intersections of race and dis/ability. *Race Ethnicity and Education*, 16(1), 1–31. Brown, L. X., Dickens, B., Gray-Garcia, T. L., Kulkarni, S. S., McLeod, L., Miller, A. L., Nusbaum, E., & Pearson, H. (2023). (Re)centering the knowledge of disabled activists, poverty scholars, and community scholars of color to transform education. *Disability Studies Quarterly*, 43(1). Kulkarni, S. S., Miller, A. L., Nusbaum, E. A., Pearson, H., & Brown, L. X. (2024). Toward disability-centered, culturally sustaining pedagogies in teacher education. *Critical Studies in Education*, 65(2), 107–127.	• Social justice lesson plans that incorporate social justice standards[3] and students taking action • Teaching philosophy assignment addressing the intersections of race, gender, ability, disability, language, and poverty • Co-facilitated or student-led IEP meetings • Co-facilitated or student-led transition and post-secondary planning/vocational support

Source: (Adapted from Kulkarni, 2021 and DCCSP Principles in Kulkarni et al., 2023)

Notes

1 https://harriettubmancollective.tumblr.com/
2 https://kriphopinstitute.com/
3 https://www.learningforjustice.org/frameworks/social-justice-standards

APPENDIX B

Table A.2 Resources for Teachers of Multiply Marginalized Disabled Students of Color

Practice	Examples	Book Chapter
Dialogic Listening	Home visits	2
	Pre-IEP meeting/chat	2
Sharing and Using Preferences	*Star Student for a Day*[1]	2
	Learning survey	2
Representation	Representative books	2
	Readings from disabled community and poverty scholars	4
		4
	Brown vs. Board and other historical lesson plans centering race and disability	6
	Representative DEI in employment opportunities	
Restorative Justice	Restorative Justice Wheel	2
	Restorative Justice Circles	3
	Modeling empathy	3
Communication	Bug and a Wish	2
	Communication journals	5
	Vision boards	5
Joyful Learning	Movement opportunities	2
		3
Honoring Student Voice	Co-create classroom expectations	3
	"Drinking Tea" dialogues	3

(Continued)

120 Appendix B

Practice	Examples	Book Chapter
Resisting Racism and Ableism	Student-led IEPs	3, 4
	Student feedback to teachers	3
	Ableism in the community	6
Direct Disability Discussions	Story Sharing	4
Belonging Connection	Educational Journey Mapping	5
	Local business partnerships based on shared interests	6

Note

1 https://www.teachingchannel.com/k12-hub/video-blog/star-student-of-the-day/

ABOUT THE AUTHORS

Samuel Bland, M.A., is a former special education teacher. He used to work at Aptitude Academy in San José, California. He earned his master's degree in special education from San José State University. He believes that students of color with disabilities should be treated with dignity and respect. Samuel believes that students of color with disabilities need teachers who engage, connect, and channel their lived experiences. He feels that it is critical that students see themselves and their cultural practices reflected in their teachers so that they may face the realities of racism and ableism. After facing some significant challenges in special education, Samuel left the field and is currently working in transportation and hospitality.

Loriann Casillas, M.A., is currently a mental health and wellbeing coordinator at Berkeley High School in Berkeley, California. She has a background as a special education elementary school teacher in Oakland, California, and strongly emphasized restorative justice in her practice. She believes that students of color with disabilities deserve equitable access to resources and inclusive learning environments.

Joanna De Leon Gaeta, M.A., is a special education teacher from San José, California. She has a bachelor's degree in literature and a minor in education from the University of California, Santa Cruz, and a master's in special education from San José State University. Being homeless and growing up in a dysfunctional and abusive household, Joanna saw education as her "ticket out" toward a brighter future. After being an instructional aide in a mild-to-moderate special education classroom, she pursued her credential and master's degree. She credits her mentor teacher, Wakeysha Taylor, for being her springboard into special education and academia. Joanna has worked in special education classrooms for a total of 11 years, spanning elementary through high school. She is currently a high school special education teacher in Oakland, California.

Ashley Highsmith-Johnson, M.A., is an education specialist at the Central Unified School District in Fresno, California. After getting her B.A. in Communication from Fresno State, she went on to receive her credential and master's degree in special education at San José State University. During her graduation ceremony, Ashley received an award for best thesis project from the special education department. She believes that students of color with disabilities deserve a fair education that provides opportunities for success both academically and in real-world contexts.

Saili S. Kulkarni, Ph.D., is Associate Professor of Special Education at San José State University. She received her doctorate in special education from the University of Wisconsin–Madison. Her research engages special education teachers of color and how they enact anti-racist, anti-ableist practices in P-12 classroom spaces. She created several affinity spaces for special education teachers of color that leaned on practical and emotional supports during the COVID-19 pandemic. Along with a team of scholars, community activists, and poverty and youth scholars across the country, Saili and her colleagues have engaged teachers in professional development experiences that center disability and race using Disability-Centered Culturally Sustaining Pedagogies (DCCSPs; Kulkarni et al., 2023). She is the recipient of a Racial Equity grant from the Spencer Foundation to study inequities across race and disability in early childhood settings. She was a former special education teacher and draws upon much of her research from her previous teaching experiences as an elementary inclusion specialist in Oakland, California.

LaVeda Harris, M.A., is a preschool special education teacher in the Los Angeles Unified School District at Annalee Elementary School in Carson, California. LaVeda is committed to breaking down systemic barriers so that students of color with disabilities can all "learn, just not in the same way or on the same day." LaVeda is a passionate advocate for children of color with disabilities and fostering environments where all children thrive. She celebrates the unique strengths and gifts of her students while advocating for equity and inclusion in education. She embraces culturally responsive, innovative practices to meet the individual needs of her students and inspire them to reach their full potentials.

INDEX

Note: Numbers in **bold** indicate a table. Numbers in *italics* indicate a figure on the corresponding page.

AANAPISIs *see* Asian American and Native American Pacific Islander-Serving Institutions
ableism: everyday 4; importance of DCCSP to unlearning 28; resistance to 58–59; in special education 103–111; in teacher education 12–27; unlearning 97–100; *see also* racism and ableism
ableist: identities 13; myth of independence 5; narratives 98; practices 105; school systems 77; special education teacher education curriculum 105; structures 17; systems 8; traditions 104; views of disability 76
abolition 91
abolitionist schooling 27
abolitionist teaching 4, 32, 45
Advanced Placement (AP) 32
Akua, C. 23
Alaskan Native or Native Hawaiian-Serving Institutions (ANNHIs) 14
Annamma, S. 4, 5, 32, 87, 105; Kulkarni's first meeting of 93
ANNHIs *see* Alaskan Native or Native Hawaiian-Serving Institutions

Antebellum South, US 103
anti-ableist education and practices 19–20, 25, 68, 78, 91, 107
anti-racist education and practices 19–20, 25, 78, 91
Ashley's story 27; Ashley's personal background and challenges in special education experienced by 94–97; Kulkarni as teacher of 93, 97–100; representative supported employment opportunities for students of color with disabilities created by 98, 99; unlearning internalized ableism and racism by 97–100; *see also* connection and community-engaged practices, summary of
Asian American and Native American Pacific Islander-Serving Institutions (AANAPISIs) 14
Artiles, A. J. 88
Atwood, A. 20

Baglieri, S. 68–69, 100, **116**
Barclay, J. L. 103
Beneke, M. R. 23, 53, 59
Ben-Moshe, L. 110
Bettini, E. 6

124 Index

Billingsley, E. 6
BIPOC *see* Black, Indigenous Peoples
 of Color
Black bodies: slavery and 103
Black early childhood special education
 (ECSE) 32
Black, Indigenous Peoples of Color
 (BIPOC) 14, 26, 103
Black joy 32–33, 105, 111; *see also* joy
 in the classroom
Blackness 103; pathologizing of 33
Bornstein, J. 13, 17, 24
Brantley-Newton, V. 37
Brantlinger, E. 13
Bristol, T. J. 14
Brown, L. X. Z. 71, **116**, **117**
Brown vs. Board of Education 70
Brunetti, G. 20

California Subject Examination for
 Teachers (CSET) test 21
CalStateTeach 52
Carrion, S. 6
Carter, P. L. 86
Carver-Thomas, D. 13
Casillas, L. *see* Loriann's story
Cheatham, G. A. 53
Cherry, M. A. 37
Cioè-Peña, M. 5, 26
confidentiality 69
connection and belonging practices,
 summary of **90**
connection and community-engaged
 practices, summary of **100–101**
connection and reframed identity,
 summary of **71**
connection and representation 36–39;
 summary of practices **38–39**
connection and restorative practices,
 summary of **56**
Connor, D. J.: open letter to the field
 of special education by 109–110;
 Urban Narratives 93, **115**, **116**
Cooc, N. 22
Cormier, C. J. 19
Council for Exceptional Children
 Conference 93
critical race studies 5
critical race theory 2; *see also* DisCrit
Cruz, R. 88
CSET *see* California Subject
 Examination for Teachers
 (CSET) test

Culturally Sustaining Pedagogies
 8; *see also* Disability-Centered
 Culturally Sustaining Pedagogies
 (DCCSPs)
Curriculum Mapping Teacher
 Education Resources on Race and
 Disability **115–118**

DCCSPs *see* Disability-Centered
 Culturally Sustaining Pedagogies
DefectCraft 103, 104
deficit-based narratives of race 4
deficit ideologies 88
deficit language 2
deficit perspectives on disability 3
deinstitutionalization of special
 education
De Leon Gaeta, J. *see* Joanna's story
Department of Education, closing of 8
dialogic listening 36–37, **38**, 45, **119**
direct disability discussions **120**
disability as: deficit 7, 13; identity 13
disabled girls of color 4; with
 complex support needs 5; in the
 school-to-prison nexus 5
disabled high school students of color
 5; *see also* young adults of color
 with disabilities
Disability-Centered Culturally
 Sustaining Pedagogies (DCCSPs) 25;
 importance to unlearning ableism of
 28; making the case for 104–105;
 principles of 69, **106**, **117**
disability-centered culturally sustaining
 practices 69
disability battle fatigue 20, 25, 91
Dis/ability critical race studies
 (DisCrit) 2–4, 19; classroom
 ecologies 20, 105; framework
 8, 23–28; Laveda and 34, 44;
 Lorianne and 58; seven tenets of 8,
 24, *106*; theory of 93
Disability Studies Critical Race Theory
 23–24
DisCrit *see* Dis/ability critical race
 studies
DisCrit-informed curriculum of teacher
 education 19; need for 4
dismantling systems of oppression
 7–8, 107
diverse children's books 37
diversity, equity, and inclusion (DEI)
double consciousness 33

"drinking tea" dialogues 56, 57, **119**
Du Bois, W. E. B. 33
Duncan-Andrade, J. 12
dysfunctional classroom ecologies 4, 104
dysfunctional educational ecologies, schools as 32
dysfunctional household 121

early childhood special education (ECSE) 32
ECSE *see* early childhood special education
Erevelles, N. 4, **116**
Erikson, E. 62
ethnoracial diversity 15
everyday ableism *see* ableism

FAPE *see* free and appropriate public education
Fenwick, L. T. 23
free and appropriate public education (FAPE) 8
Fritsch, K. 37

Gage, N. A. 86
Gifted and Talented Education programs 32
Gist, C. D. 14
Gray-Garcia, T. (Tiny) 80
Grow Your Own programs 14

Harris, L. *see* Laveda's story
Harry, B. 4, 104
HBCUs *see* Historically Black Colleges
Highsmith-Johnson, A. *see* Ashley's story
Hispanic-Serving Institutions (HSIs) 14
Historically Black Colleges (HBCUs) 14
homelessness 52, 81, 110
honoring student voice 52, 55–57, 60, **119**
HSIs *see* Hispanic-Serving Institutions
humanizing behavior and communication practices **43–44**
Hurston, Z. N. 7; *How It Feels to Be Colored Me* 111; Stewart's book on 105, 111
hypersurveillance 32

IDEA *see* Individuals with Disabilities Education Act
IEP *see* Individualized Education Plan

IFSP *see* Individualized Family Support Plan
imposter syndrome 66–68, 77
Individualized Education Plan (IEP) 12, 49–51, **71–72**; co-generating **115**; compliance with 65, 84; goals 87; pre-IEP **38**, **119**; self-monitoring during meetings 70; student led 56, **117**, **120**; undertraining in 95
Individualized Family Support Plan (IFSP) 49
Individuals with Disabilities Education Act (IDEA) 8
intersectional identities 15, 26, 70
Invalid, S. 5
Irizarry, J. 55

Jacks, L. L. 88
Joanna's story 27, 77, 80–91; background and personal history of 81–83; challenges in as teacher in special education faced by 83–84; classroom behaviors and challenges observed by 84–86; homelessness and trauma experienced by 27; Kulkarni's analysis of classroom observations by 86–91; writing of a book chapter with Kulkarni and Samuel 77; *see also* connection and belonging; male minority students
joy in the classroom 8, 42–45, *105*, 107, **119**

Kaba, M. 91
Kafka, J. 13
Klingner, J. 4, 5, 104
Kohli, R. 33, 104
Kulkarni, S. ("Saili") 24, 59, 62; Ashley's story shared by 93, 97–100; first meeting of Annamma by 93; Joanna's classroom observations analyzed by 86–91; Laveda' s story shared by 32–34, 44–45; Loriann's story shared by 51–52; Samuel's writing of a book chapter with Joanne and 77; Samuel's story shared by 66–68

Ladson-Billings, G.: *Dreamkeepers* 26
Lalvani, P. 68–69, 100
LaVeda's story 27, 32–45; ClassDojo used by 37; dialogic listening by

36–37, **38**, 45; diverse books read
in the classroom of 37; integrating
connection and representation
by 36–39; Kulkarni's analysis of
32–34, 44–45; personal background
and history of 34–35; Replacement
Skills Teaching by 40, *41*, 42
Leko, M. M. 100
Linton, S. 99
Loriann's story 27, 48–60, 103,
107–108; challenges of special
education teaching for 49–51;
honoring of student voice by
52, 55–57, 60; exit from special
education by 111; how she became
an elementary school teacher 49;
Kulkarni's narrative of 51–52;
restorative justice practices for
students of color with disabilities
utilized by 52–60; whiteness
decentered by 108; *see also*
restorative justice lens
Love, B. 4, 32
Love, H. R. 23

male minority students: Black and
Brown 82; discipline disparities
among 86; humanizing practices
for 86–88; Joanna's work with 85,
91, 108
Mansfield, K. C. 55
McLean, M. 76
MEBS *see* Multi-Element Behavior
Support
Meiners, E. R. 80
mentor of color 17
Miller, A. L. 4, 5, **115, 117**
Minority-Serving Institutions (MSIs) 2,
14–15, 23, 36
Moore, L. 75–76; *Black Disabled Art
History* 75
Morales, A. R. 15
Morrison, D. 4, 32, 105
MSIs *see* Minority-Serving Institutions
MTSS *see* Multi-Tiered Systems of
Support (MTSS) process
multiply marginalized disabled students
of color 3–4, 18, 111; actively
building resistance and cultivating
joy with 105–108; centering 110;
deficit views of 45; Joanna's work
with 80; LaVeda's dedication

to 45; Samuel's support for 77;
Resources for Teachers of Multiply
Marginalized Disabled Students of
Color **120–121**; school-to-prison
nexus of 110; teachers working
across the P-12 span in California of
26; as term 8n1
multiply marginalized students with
disabilities 5, 58
Multi-Element Behavior Support
(MEBS) 39–40, 42
Multi-Tiered Systems of Support
(MTSS) process 39

Native American Non-Tribal
Institutions (NANTIs) 14
Nusbaum, E. 4, 5, **116, 117**

old boys club 13
"only, the" 50, 59, 60, 93, 94, 96, 98,
101, 102

Parmar, J. 5
Patel, L. 1
PBIs *see* Predominantly Black
Institutions
Perlow, O. 32
Poor Magazine 80
Poor Press 80
Predominantly Black Institutions
(PBIs) 14
President's Commission on Special
Education: *A New Era: Revitalizing
Special Education for Children and
Their Families* 15
psychosocial development, theory of 62

racism and ableism 8, 58; DisCrit Tenet
One on 24; in special education
103–111; resisting 6, **120**; in
teacher education 12–28; undoing
3; *see also* unlearning racism and
ableism
Regional Educational Laboratory of
Education Northwest 15
resistance not resilience 108–111
restorative justice 27, 53–54, **119**
restorative justice lens 52, 57–58, 60
restorative justice practices for students
of color with disabilities 39, 50, 51,
52–60
Resource Program (RSP) 49, **56**

Response to Intervention (RTI) process 39
restorative justice as lens 57–58
right-wing agendas 8
Roberts, C. 62, **100**
RTI *see* Response to Intervention (RTI) process

Samuel's story 27, 62–78; background and personal history of 63–66; Kulkarni on Samuel's experiencing of imposter syndrome 66–68; navigation of identity by 68–70; sample lesson plan shared by 70–76
Santa Clara County 64; Office of Education 63
Scott, L. A. 18–19, 23
SETOC *see* special education teachers of color
Siuty, M. B. 20, 24, 104
Skiba, R. J. 16
Special Day Class (SDC) 49
special education: President's Commission on Special Education 15; racism and racist imperatives of 13, 24; reducing disproportionality in 17
Special Education credentialing process 21–22
Special Education teachers of color (SETOC) 19–20, 24–25; narratives of 25–26; California as context for 20–23; challenges faced. by 49–51; DisCrit framework for 23–28; research on the experiences of 15–20; understanding racism and ableism through 12–28; white women and 24
Spring, J. 91
spirit murder 7
Star Student of the Day video 36
Stewart, L.: *The Politics of Joy* 105, 111
student voice *see* honoring student voice

Taylor, W. 122
TCUs *see* Tribal Colleges or Universities
Teacher Education Advancement for a Multicultural Society (TEAMS/ AmeriCorps) 12
teacher preparation programs, "urban" 104

teachers of color: recruiting and educating 13–14; *see also* SETOC
TEAMS/AmeriCorps *see* Teacher Education Advancement for a Multicultural Society (TEAMS/ AmeriCorps)
Tefera, A. 103–104
Thornton, B. 18
Title III of the Higher Education Act of 1965
Trainor, A. A. 17
Tribal Colleges or Universities (TCUs) 14
Trump, D. J. 8
Tyler, N. C. 18

University of California, Santa Cruz 82
unlearning racism and ableism 7, 28, 93, 104, 107; unlearning internalized racism and ableism 97; unlearning racism and ableism with high school students 97–100

Villegas, A. M. 14
vision boards 87, *88*, *89*, **119**
Voltz, D. L. 16

West, C. 93
whiteness: Blackness contrasted to 103; decentering 5, **39**; dominant ideologies of participation and behavior in schools and 89; privileging of 45
whiteness and ability 3; as property 24
whiteness and ableism: adherence to 33; decentering 25, 54, 104
whiteness and racism: institutional 13; decentering 22; technocratic upholding of 23
white saviorism complex 3, 104
white women as teachers 13, 16–17, 20, 24, 93, 104
Winn, M. T. 80
Wong, A.: *Disability Visibility* 1, 102

Yang, M. 22
young adults 95, 97
young adults of color with disabilities 98, 100
young adults with disabilities 76